THE LORD'S CREED

THE LORD'S CREED

by

GEORGE INGLE

Bishop of Willesden

COLLINS

St James's Place, London

1964

To Mary my wife

© *George Ingle, 1964*
Printed in Great Britain
Collins Clear-Type Press
London and Glasgow

Contents

Author's Note

HOW MUCH this book owes to others will be obvious. I can only express my gratitude by saying that I do not know the extent of my debt, for the influence of others goes much deeper than memory. Thus if I have omitted to acknowledge some ideas and expressions I offer my apology. I have quoted very freely and make no apology for doing so, for two reasons. First it is right in attempting this work to draw widely on the wisdom and experience of others. Secondly, I have bought and read many a book because I have been attracted by quotations from them in other works. Others may reap at least this reward from reading mine.

Unless otherwise stated, biblical quotations from the Old Testament are taken from the Revised Standard Version, and those from the New Testament from the New English Bible.

George Willesden

I. LORD, TEACH US TO PRAY

Multitudes, multitudes in the valley of decision!   Joel 3:14

Perhaps people are beginning to understand that we can no longer afford the luxury of scepticism, that we must start again believing in belief.
                    Lindsay Anderson in *Declaration*, p. 176

It is not only what is said that matters, but also the man who says it.
                    Dietrich Bonhoeffer, *Ethics*, p. 238

Here I stand knocking at the door; if anyone hears my voice and opens the door, I will come in.
                    Revelation 2: 30

His (Jesus') words had electrified his hearers. His doctrines had pierced to the heart through all the coats and layers of human selfishness and blindness.
                    Lord Beaverbrook, *The Divine Propagandist*, p. 2

MANY PEOPLE are wondering what they can believe, and how much, if anything, of traditional values and morals have survived and deserve to survive. Their doubts are fostered by the literature of rejection in which the sceptics and the rebels maintain that we are carrying the lumber of the past and the sooner we are rid of it the better. But there is also the literature of recovery and it is refreshing to be told that the first step in recovery is to believe in belief.

It is a commonplace that our material progress has outrun our moral and spiritual development. The real

7

difference between this and preceding ages can be summed up in one word, power. New discoveries mean more power, more power means more responsibility, and there is no doubt that God is trusting us to-day as men have never been trusted before. Looking at things in this way we ought to talk much more about opportunities, less about problems, for every new discovery is a gift from God and every one of his gifts an opportunity for great good. But how can we hope to use them aright, unless we believe that because they are his gifts he alone can show us the way?

"Doctrine draws with it conduct in harmony with itself," wrote Bishop Hensley Henson, and no truer words were written. There is no doctrine behind the advance in the application of science and therefore no sense of purpose. We are not even asking the right questions, let alone finding the right answers. We are obsessed with what we can do, we do not stop to ask what we ought to do and whether we ought to do all we can do. There is no escape from becoming the slaves of things except through doctrine, because doctrine and conduct are inseparable. There is nothing sillier than the popular "It doesn't matter what you believe so long as you do what is right." In recent times two pernicious doctrines have led to appalling treatment of millions of people— Hitler's Master Race and Communism. Both have been taught and practised as doctrines with religious fervour and it is this fact which has made them so dangerous and which is so dangerous to ignore.

Doctrine draws with it conduct in harmony with itself; and therefore it is vital that belief should be based on theology, for theology relates both creed and conduct to God. Doctrine without theology is doctrine without

God and that is even more dangerous than no doctrine at all. There are two sorts of enemy of progress and they both ignore the Sin of the world. One expects everyone to behave as if human nature is perfect and the conditions of life ideal; the other makes no such assumption, but believes that we are capable of raising ourselves by our own boot-strings. The one ignores the facts of life, the other the need for a Power beyond our own. There is no final solution of problems whilst sin remains, but we have to do the best we can in the world as it is, neither ignoring the obvious fact that human nature is far from perfect nor condoning or acquiescing in evil, least of all in ourselves. We have to do all we can to eradicate evil and at the same time to alter conditions and circumstances which encourage and perpetuate it. This is, quite literally, a superhuman task, but it is not beyond the range of responsible human effort and will inspired and directed by God.

Responsibility is corporate as well as personal and the Church should be the corporate body *par excellence*, the responsible society, for it owes its allegiance to one Lord and Master and derives its life from him. It is the agent through which he continues his work; thus the Church can claim to be the Body of Christ on earth and we to be members of it. Hence its responsibilities are enormous, its sphere of influence potentially limitless, its privileges glorious. Some realisation of this is surely reflected in the disciple's request: " Lord, teach *us* to pray." He was one of a corporate band of followers and spoke for all. At any rate the answer he got was a corporate answer, for every clause in the Lord's Creed is in the plural. But we are faced with the sad situation of a divided Church: and our divisions are not only between

Churches, but often within the same Church. This inevitably cripples the work and particularly corporate action. Allegiance to *a* Church, or even to a party in that Church, comes before allegiance to Christ. Sometimes the result is that people concentrate on saving their own souls, quite forgetting that community is of the very essence of Christianity and that Jesus is the Saviour of the *world*.

The World Church is a fact and is the greatest power for good in the world to-day. Here in England we need constantly to remind ourselves that the Church of England is the Established Church of the land, the National Church, and as such is so bound up with our corporate life, our character, our institutions and our laws that no one can easily assess what we owe to this relationship, still less what would be the result if it were severed. Deposited in the Church is the stored-up experience of the ages and there is a great body of doctrine which rests upon the authority of the Church. " The Church to teach, the Bible to prove " has always been the standpoint of the Church of England. The average layman knows little of the doctrine and is often reluctant to accept the authority. He cannot be saddled with all the blame, for the Church has not always been a good teacher and the very comprehensiveness of the Church of England leaves a great deal to individual conscience and judgment. The laity should be grateful that it does, but realise that it throws a corresponding responsibility on them. They have to overcome their innate antipathy to doctrine, for the Englishman is a pragmatist, a man of deeds, not words, still less of abstract speculations.

It may be, however, that there is more readiness to-day to see the fallacy of this attitude. Millions of people hear and see on television discussions on politics, morals, philosophy and religion, and some must begin to see that belief is relevant to conduct. There is also plenty of evidence before us of what happens when men hold certain beliefs, or none at all—the results of Apartheid in Africa or of Communism in the Satellite States, the challenge to constitutional government by the Committee of 100, violence from race discrimination, the antics of the beatniks and the teddy boys, and the effect on society if people not only break the moral absolutes but deny that there are any. In this way the media of communication can do a great deal to persuade people that it does matter what a man believes. The danger is, of course, that the result may so easily become indoctrination, for the hidden persuaders of voice and vision are immensely powerful, and sometimes utterly unscrupulous. Communication can sharpen our critical faculties, awaken conscience and give us the material on which to make responsible decisions; or it can lull us into a passive acceptance of the opinions of others, with a heavy premium on the popular idol of the moment. But that is a risk we have to take; all the more reason why the Church should take a much larger share in the use of the modern means of communication, since for every person who hears a sermon there must be thousands who use television.

If conduct depends on doctrine and doctrine on faith, we shall avoid the error which St. Paul attacks in Romans. Our whole theme is that " works " depend on faith. But faith is not purely instinctive. It is " instinct illuminated by reason "[1]; and " reason " must not be limited to what is called the scientific method. It must

[1] *The Philosophy of the Good Life*, Gore, p. 285.

embrace in its meaning all that is implied in understanding. William Temple, in discussing "the Perils of a purely Scientific Education," [1] says that there are two kinds of understanding, one that can be gained in the laboratory, another—applicable only to human beings—which comes from sympathy. In human relationships the latter is far more important than the scientific method. (Perhaps this is what Wordsworth meant when he wrote of

> a fingering slave,
> one that would peep and botanize
> upon his mother's grave.)

When St. Paul says we are justified by faith and not by works, "it is made very clear that works include religious works. . . . The most direct and comprehensive statement of the very same point is to be found in the Hymn in Praise of Love in I. Cor. 13." [2] This needs saying because every parish priest, and especially anyone who deals with prospective ordinands, has met people who want to do "full-time church work," sometimes to the neglect of family commitments and demanding more sacrifice from others than from themselves. If marriage and the upbringing of children, together with a Christian witness in a secular job in a difficult world, is not full-time church work, then what is? One of the greatest books ever written is open to the same criticism—"The Pilgrim's Progress from this World to That which is to come under the Similitude of a Dream." It is not a pilgrimage in and through the world but an escape *from* the world, and it starts with the shocking spectacle of a man deserting his wife and children and putting his

[1] In *Religious Experience*, p. 168.
[2] *Beyond Religion*, Daniel Jenkins, p. 41.

fingers in his ears that he may not hear their cries. We can never escape from conduct in community, and therefore moral conduct must mean sympathetic relations with people and acknowledgment of our duty towards them. Nothing requires more rational, sympathetic understanding than this. It is the second great commandment, but we cannot obey it unless we obey the first. Both commandments are centred on God and they are the essence of the creed of Jesus Christ.

The starting point is prayer and within the reach of everyone. Many people never pray at all and may not know what they are missing, or, more important still, how the lives they touch are missing something. They are satisfied. But if we think of sin, not just in terms of misdemeanour, but as separation from God, " a man does not have to be unfaithful to his wife or dishonest in his dealings, or anti-social in any other way in order to be a sinner. He has only to be satisfied with himself." [1] Some who do not pray are not satisfied with life or with themselves. There is a vacuum in their lives and they may be just plainly bored. There are others who pray, but use no formal prayers and keep no set times: perhaps some of them know more about prayer than many who do. " Working is praying " is often an excuse for not praying at all or for an undisciplined life. But not always, for there are some whose work is a living prayer. Nevertheless we need to remind ourselves that prayer is work, often the hardest work of all.

Strangely enough, those who do pray are rarely satisfied with themselves or their prayers. But not really strange, for to pray at all makes us want to grow better and to pray better. Lord, teach us to pray. Why are our

[1] *The Plain Man Looks at Himself*, W. Purcell, p. 18.

prayers not better? Is it that we bring so little into them that we take so little out of them? Is it that they are too formal, made up of other people's thoughts and words and so not really touching the life we have to live? "There is a type of thinking which remains safely at home, merely receiving reports, maps and photographs of what lies beyond the garden wall, and speculates, often with great cleverness, on the basis of such dispatches received. Thinking and living are thus divorced, or rather, thinking is made into the instrument of escape from involvement with life. Why dive into the sea if you can talk about it so well and think about it so clearly? But in such circumstances the object of thought becomes no more than an imaginary toy. That is why much talk about God cuts no ice. What is talked about has never been lived." [1] So it is with much of our praying; we neither pray what we live nor live what we pray. But for some it is different and they are generally those who feel so keenly the sin and suffering of the world that they can say, " Out of the deep have I called unto thee, O Lord: Lord hear my voice." [2] These are they who " going through the vale of misery use it for a well: and the pools are filled with water." [3] There is a clergyman who, when he celebrates the Holy Communion, places his diary upon the altar. An empty gesture? No, a symbolic act, a dedication and a prayer that God will
> direct, control, suggest, this day
> all I design, or do, or say.

He is a man to whom all sorts of people come with their sorrows and sins and problems. Their names are

---

[1] "Theology and Self Awareness," H. A. Williams in *Soundings*, p. 73.

[2] Psalm 130: 1.   [3] Psalm 84: 6.

scrawled in his diary, their burdens written on his heart.

We do not know who said to Jesus, " Lord, teach us to pray." He was just one of his disciples. The occasion was when " once, in a certain place, Jesus was at prayer."[1] This was not by any means the first time they had seen him praying; they had even known him to spend a whole night in prayer [2]; and of course they prayed themselves. But they already knew Jesus well enough to be sure that if anyone could help them to pray better, he could. The man who asked the question is Everyman; he spoke for us all. But we ought to be profoundly grateful to him, for he got far more than he asked for or expected. The Lord's Prayer is not just a prayer; it is also, as Father Andrew says, the Lord's own Creed. Therefore it is infinitely more important than any man-made creed. Belief is based on experience, our own and the inherited experience of the ages. The Lord's Creed is unique because his experience of God and his relationship to God were unique.

Believing and praying are always closely linked together, but here they are so close that when we use the prayer we are committing ourselves to a creed. Hence of all prayers it is the easiest to *say*, the most difficult to *pray*. It can either be a mere form of words or a perpetual discovery and challenge. It is both comforting and disturbing—comforting because it throws light on our problems and points the way to their solution, disturbing because it challenges us to responsibility and decision.

St. Augustine said, " Believe in order that you may understand." This is precisely what Jesus meant when

[1] Luke 11: 1.   [2] Luke 6: 12.

he gave us his prayer. Here we are taught to pray and believe by the One who has unique authority to tell us the truth about God and man, for in him we see the whole of humanity and the whole of God. Here then belief, prayer and action are all one and all directed by the one supreme reality that the Kingdom, the Power and the Glory belong to God alone.

This is not a book on prayer or simply on prayer in the Lord's Prayer. It is an attempt to show the Lord's Creed in the Lord's Prayer. To suggest that any one person can discover all the implications of that creed would be absurd. One can only hope that what is here written may help others to discover more. There is only one purpose throughout this book—" that we may live more nearly as we pray."

> Dear Master, in whose life I see
> All that I would, but fail to be,
> Let thy clear light for ever shine,
> To shame and guide this life of mine.
>
> Though what I dream and what I do
> In my weak days are always two,
> Help me, oppressed by things undone,
> O thou, whose deeds and dreams were one! [1]

[1] John Hunter in *The Public School Hymn Book.*

II. OUR FATHER

" God is love " . . . is to be read with the emphasis on the word God, whereas we have fallen into the habit of emphasising the word love. *God* is love. . . . Only he who knows God knows what love is; it is not the other way round.

Dietrich Bonhoeffer, Ethics, p. 173

He that hath seen me, hath seen the Father. John 14: 9. Those are the words we long to hear. . . . In adoration, in supplication, in dedication, let us take care always to address ourselves to God as he is seen in Jesus Christ. Never ask in prayer for any blessing till you are sure your mind is turned to Jesus Christ; then speak to God as you see him there.

William Temple, Readings in St. John's Gospel, p. 233

There is no such thing as a " christian ideology " . . . Christianity is not an ideology generating a religion, but a religion in search of a social expression.

Alan Richardson, Christian Apologetics, pp. 87, 71

The real menace to life in the world to-day is not the hydrogen bomb . . . but the fact of proximity without community.

Murdo Ewen Macdonald, The Need to Believe, p. 82

THE WORDS "Our father" rank amongst the great sayings of the world, for they express our profoundest belief about the very nature of God. They must stand side by side with the first four words of the Bible, " In the beginning God." The latter must be the foundation or doctrine on which all science and technology are built, if man's achievements are to have any meaning and purpose at all; the former must be the foundation or doctrine of all human institutions, if they are to survive and not to disintegrate into anarchy and chaos. " Father " is not an easy word to describe because it is so much part of our lives that we find no need to express its meaning. We can, however, say that it means for us love, dependence and security.

First then, love. A father's love must be love with discipline and the two are not incompatible; in fact they are inseparable. Real love must have its sterner side; it must serve the best interests of the loved one and therefore it cannot encourage weaknesss or condone wrong-doing. Love without discipline becomes indulgence, and parents who spoil their children just do not love them enough because they are really hurting them and spoiling their characters. They give them immediate temporary pleasures at the expense of happiness in the future, and incidentally they are storing up grief and pain for themselves. St. Paul speaks of the " kindness and severity of God," [1] and the Psalmist of his " mercy and judgment."[2] Lots of people think of the love of Our Father in terms of indulgent parents. God to them is like the " good fellow " in Omar Khayyám.

" Why," said another, " some there are who tell
Of one who threatens he will toss to hell
The luckless pots he marred in making.
Pish! He's a good fellow and 'twill all be well."

But Our Father is not like that. He is the true Father whose love is such that it dares to discipline and punish.

Secondly, there is dependence, but it must be dependence with freedom. To begin with the child is completely dependent on his parents and in the earliest stages mostly on the mother. Later on he sees his father

[1] Romans 11 : 22.   [2] Psalm 101 : 1.

as head of the family, his counsellor and guide. But the wise father gradually gives him more and more freedom; he will not be afraid to let him grow up. But still there is dependence, not that of childhood, but the adult dependence of friendship and companionship based on love and mutual respect. This ideal relationship between father and son is unhappily not always achieved, but when it is it becomes the human counterpart of our relationship with God our Father. There is the same dependence with freedom. In him we live and move and have our being. We can never be independent of him because we are bound to him by his love for us and our love for him. But because the tie is the tie of love, he gives us freedom and he respects our freedom so much that we can break that tie. That is a solemn thought, but human experience tells us that it is true; for every father knows that he cannot control his son's destiny; every child is free to choose.

Thirdly, security, but security with responsibility. The home is security. Whatever happens in the world outside we can go home and find sympathy and understanding. But it cannot be all take and no give. Just because we find so much in home and family, we are responsible for it, we are all members one of another. The very freedom which we enjoy is dependent on our behaving as responsible people. We cannot have freedom and security without this condition. Because we are free to choose we must take reponsibility for our choices and we must accept the consequences of them. Again this is the human copy of God's pattern for his children. He has never promised material security, but as Our Father he offers us the security of love, sympathy and understanding: that inner security which is described in a prayer—" the royalty of inward happiness and the serenity of living close to thee." But nothing he gives us is to be selfishly enjoyed. We are responsible to God for ourselves, for others, for the gifts and talents he gives us. The last thing we can hope for is security without responsibility: for that would mean renouncing our obligations as children of the family of God and refusing the one condition on which we can have freedom.

This age is often called the age of insecurity. The surprising thing is that the sense of insecurity coincides with unprecedented material prosperity. If we look for the causes of this feeling of insecurity, we can find some of them in the instability of home and family life, the restlessness and pace of life, the never-ceasing process of creating more and more wants, and perhaps the fear of nuclear war. But none of these touches the heart of the matter. The one obvious fact stands out a mile. There never has been and never will be a material security which can completely satisfy and supply all man's needs. Gastric ulcers are the occupational disease of the wealthy business tycoon and hooliganism is rampant amongst the youngsters who have more to spend than they have ever had before. The connection between insecurity and loss of faith is too obvious to need emphasising. Men are without security because they are without God in the world.

It is for this reason that many people are willing to sacrifice the responsibility of freedom for the security of dependence. Some want to be relieved of the bother of thinking for themselves, so they submit to the authority of fundamentalism or the Roman Catholic Church. Others expect everything to be handed to them on a plate by a benevolent Welfare State. They have no faith in

God, but readily accept the popular creed, " Science teaches." They need, but they do not know it, a God who is their Father, a home in which there is love with discipline, dependence with freedom, security with responsibility.

But we have to face the possibility that some people may find it not a help but a hindrance to think of God as Father. In the comfortable Victorian home father was a remote, often a stern, figure. He was rarely seen by his children and when he was seen he might be addressed as " Sir ". In fact the relationship between father and children might be precisely the opposite of what the word " father " is meant to convey—no warmth or tenderness or expression of love. God is in his heaven like father in his study, unapproachable by his children. This picture is, of course, out of date, but there are others which are not. There are plenty of children who do not know their fathers and plenty who know them only too well. Suppose father is an autocrat in the home and everyone must bow to his will. Suppose father is a drunkard or goes off with another woman and deserts the home after years of quarrels and bickerings with mother. The child sees all this; he sees his mother's misery. How can he love and respect his father who has shown no love and respect for him? How can it help him to be told that God is like a father? This is a real difficulty, but it cannot be solved by abandoning " Our Father". Indeed it is the father-vacuum in a child's life that the Fatherhood of God can fill. Whatever his experience has been, a child knows instinctively that he should have a real father and, although he may be embittered, he will respond to love; and he can be taught that God is love. To him " God is Father " and " God is Love " are not yet the same thing. But let him start with " God is love " and perhaps one day the bitterness of " father " will be purged away and he will resolve to be a real father to his own children.

We have already touched on a second difficulty. We said that children *instinctively* know that they should have a father. Yes, says the psychologist, and that is why they make their own Father-God. He is an image of their own imagination, a prop for their weakness, a fantasy of dependence when they ought to grow up to be independent. Just as children depend on their parents, so grown-up children make a God on whom they can lean. Sartre pushes this argument to its logical conclusion and turns the parable of the Prodigal Son on its head. The son was quite right to leave his home. He was seeking independence and revolting against being tied to his father. There are some half-truths in all this. First, it is perfectly true that we describe the character of God in human terms. When we call him " Father " we are employing a human image. The technical word for this is anthropomorphism, which means to make God in the likeness of man. We cannot help doing this because we have no other means of describing him. But it is one thing to use human terms and images to describe God, quite another to confine him to the limitations which they imply. We are simply doing the best we can with the language and expressions available. The very fact that God became man in Jesus shows that God expressed himself in human form because in no other way could we see and know what God is like. We can never comprehend God for he is infinite and we finite. But we can apprehend something of his glory and love and power in Jesus Christ. When we come to consider " Who art in Heaven " we shall see that " Father " does not exhaust the full meaning of God, but that it does speak to us of his loving care and his presence with us.

Secondly, it is again true that every child must grow up, stand on his own legs and leave his home. There are plenty of tragedies in the world through possessive parents and mother- or father-tied children. Wise parents know this. They try to bring up their children as responsible beings and yet always to make a home where the security of love is to be found. The dependence of childhood passes into the relationship of love and respect and significance. There is always the risk that the transition may be revolt, that love will be spurned. God himself takes this risk. This is what the Parable of the Prodigal Son describes. The father made no attempt to force his son to stay in the home, but he never stopped loving him. And when the son came to his senses the father met him when he was a long way off, and—mark you—took him back, not as a hired servant, but as a free son.

But the real fallacy is in the suggestion that we make a Father-God because we instinctively feel the need for a father. We can very easily turn the tables on this and say that it is precisely because we have this instinct that it is rooted in reality and is meant to be and can be satisfied. If it were not so, it would be the only instinct that cannot be satisfied and is based on illusion. The instinct of self-preservation tells us how to keep alive. Hunger, thirst and fear are signals which have to be obeyed. This instinct to preserve self passes into the higher one to preserve life and in obeying it men again and again have sacrificed their own lives. The maternal instinct is so obviously real that it needs no justification.

But we can still marvel to see birds and animals scorning danger and doing the most fantastic things to protect their young. The sex instinct ensures that the human race, like every other species, continues and does not die out. It is part of the creative instinct in man which is responsible for the arts and crafts and all the manifold achievements of man. At its highest it is creative co-operation with the will of God. Are we really asked to believe that man's instinctive longing for a Father-God is an illusion, is the only instinct which cannot be satisfied in reality? Surely that is too much. It is far more reasonable to believe that there is a religious instinct in man and that to call God Father is part of the fulfilment of it. This is a valid assumption and there is further evidence to support it.

The objection we have noted is serious because it would not only invalidate the idea of a Father-God, but also the fundamental belief that God discloses himself to man. It does in fact deny that there is any religious instinct at all. Thus

it is proposed to explain, or explain away, the impression to which the human conscience has so widely surrendered itself, of being in contact with a God who knows it and would communicate himself to it, by psychological considerations. Thus the experience of answers to prayer is resolved into self-suggestion, and self-revelation of God into " uprushes from the subconscious." . . . But we can recognise that the whole of the human advance, alike nature-ward, man-ward, and God-ward, has been based on a fundamental faith natural to man, that his instinctive assumptions are not purely delusive but bring

him into contact with reality; and it is very difficult
to affirm the reality of nature and the trustworthiness
of natural science while refusing to recognise the
reality of the spiritual values inherent in nature and
the divine activity upon the soul of man, to both of
which the human conscience bears convincing
witness.

But we may go farther than that: we may point
out that the subconscious region of man's mind,
while it is or may be the depository of a vast amount
of animal and sub-human instincts and " racial
memories " and mental experience, which prudence
or pride has forced us to suppress, has provided no
evidence at all worthy of the name to show that it
can be the source of new knowledge or fresh disclos-
ures such as have advanced and ennobled man. . . .
It is the active conscious mind or will or heart which
appears to have the credit for the ideas and discoveries which have advanced mankind. There is no
justification for attributing to " the subconscious "
the thoughts and utterances of Amos or Isaiah or
Jesus. There was nothing in their past traditions to
account for such thoughts. It must be acknowledged
that they have all the appearance of being down-
rushes from the superconscious rather than uprushes
from below the level.[1]

A similar conclusion in another context is reached by
Lord Beaverbrook who does not claim to be a theologian:

Nature, working under the Providence of God, does
not bestow instincts on her creatures and at the same
time refuse to satisfy them. Looked at from one

[1] Gore, *The Philosophy of the Good Life*, 270–2.

point of view nature is the fulfilment of instinct. When, therefore, the sceptic suggests that we cheat ourselves in this matter, consciously or unconsciously, and believe in immortality because we wish to have it so, he is really putting forward one of the strongest arguments in favour of future existence. It is the very strength of this idea for perpetuation which is the best proof that the promise of Jesus will be fulfilled.[1]

We have dealt with this objection at some length because it lies at the root of much doubt and scepticism and may lead to disbelief. Incidentally it brings no credit to the comparatively young science of psychology which can be of immense service to the understanding of the human mind and of human behaviour. The conclusion then is, not only that we can trust our instinctive belief that God is a loving Father, but that this instinct is one of the strongest " proofs " of the existence of a Father-God.

But he is *Our* Father. We must not use the word " Father " in isolation. These two simple familiar words are the very heart of the Lord's Creed. They establish a condition without which we can neither pray the prayer nor understand its creed. The Lord's Prayer is a corporate, family prayer. Every clause, every petition is in the plural. *Our* Father, not my Father; give *us*, not me, *our* daily bread; forgive *us* as *we* forgive; lead *us* not into temptation but deliver *us* from evil. We can of course pray in the singular, for each one of us must bring his needs—and his sins—to God. We can even do so in the Lord's Prayer, but only if we remember that

[1] *The Divine Propagandist*, 54-5.

we are members of the family of God, bearing our share of responsibility for it, acknowledging our share of the Sin of the world and ready to share with others the blessings we enjoy. Thus right at the start of the Lord's Prayer we are told quite plainly that we are members one of another, that human life is lived in society and that we can only enjoy the privileges of corporate life if we accept the responsibilities; we cannot have bread or forgiveness or security from evil unless we are just as eager that others should have them too. Here is a doctrine and a very searching one. We cannot escape it, and if we say " Our Father " and are not prepared to accept its implications, we cannot go any further with this prayer.

The Lord's Prayer is a corporate prayer because it is *the* Family Prayer. It was no new thing to call God Father. There are plenty of instances in the Old Testament of this. But what Jesus did was to establish the *family principle* as God's way of governing the world. Because God is Father and all we his children, life must be ordered on the family principle; and by his life on earth and in his teaching Jesus put the divine stamp on the human institution of the family. Jesus came as a baby born of his mother; he lived and grew up in a home and for thirty years he lived in that home, working and supporting the family. Many of his parables and illustrations were drawn from home-life and they are just the kind which ordinary simple folk would appreciate and understand. The marriage service reminds us that Holy Matrimony is an " honourable estate, instituted of God " and that this " holy estate Christ adorned and beautified with his presence, and first miracle that he wrought, in Cana of Galilee." Thus one of the first recorded acts of Christ was to go to a wedding reception and there to do something which was not simply a wonderful act to remedy an embarrassing situation, but a sign or symbol of eternal truth, the difference that Christ can make, turning the ordinary things of life into something far richer and fuller, and the occasion was the beginning of a new home and family life. Equally significant is the incident when parents brought their children to be blessed. " Let the little ones come to me," he said, " do not try to stop them," [1] and there are no more terrible words in the whole Bible than his condemnation of anyone who causes a little one to stumble.[2] Could there be a clearer indictment of those who cause the breakdown of family life? Would not these words give pause to anyone contemplating divorce? Then there is the final gracious, loving touch when, in the midst of his agony on the cross, Jesus thought of his mother's grief and desolation and consigned her to the care of his disciple and friend.[3]

Here then is the doctrine of the family in the Lord's Creed. Life organised on the family principle is life in accord with the divine purpose and everything which runs counter to it will, not may, lead to disaster and chaos. It is, of course, strictly in accord with human experience. Common sense alone would argue that a human institution which has stood the test of time is clearly the basis of all human society and that we tamper with it at our peril. But when we can see that the idea of the human family is rooted in God and that the family principle is a divine principle, it is madness to ignore the threats to it.

That there are danger signals is obvious, but we must

[1] Luke 18 : 16.   [2] Luke 17 : 2.   [3] John 19 : 25-7.

be careful not to get a distorted picture. It is commonly
held that to-day family life is unstable, and sometimes it
is implied that it is more unstable than in former times.
Both views can be challenged.[1] " Englishmen are always
despondent about their own times, and it would be easy
to quote contemporaries in every period so that their
testimony would show that we had gone downhill ever
since the time of the Norman Conquest." [2] Concern
about home and family life and our anxiety about the
fifth and seventh commandments " ought not to betray
us into breaches of the ninth; for the Word of God is as
strong to defend the integrity of our neighbour's reputa-
tion as it is to protect his family ties. ' Thou shalt not
bear false witness against thy neighbour '." [3] This is
a timely reminder, for there is an obligation to face all
the facts, and there are facts which give cause for hope
rather than despondency.

Great changes have taken place in family life and we
have yet to see the outcome of them. " We have made
it (marriage) at one and the same time potentially more
rewarding and potentially more unstable," [4] and it would
be stupid to assume that the worst will happen. Indeed,
compared with times past, home and family life to-day
may be fuller, more rewarding and even more stable.
Again, although there are disruptive influences at work,
there is evidence that many people are facing these with
wisdom and a sense of responsibility; and even if their
first effect may be to disrupt, they can be used to form

[1] See *The Family is not Broken*, G. R. Dunstan, and the Penguin
Special, *Britain in the Sixties—The Family and Marriage*, Ronald
Fletcher.

[2] L. C. A. Knowles, quoted by Fletcher, op. cit., p. 9.

[3] Dunstan, op. cit., p. 7.

[4] Fletcher, op. cit., p. 130.

a new pattern of family life which is stable and sound. It is only fair to add that a good deal of the misbehaviour of youngsters to-day can be traced to causes which lie in the past and that already the present holds out better hopes for the future. For example, " Earlier generations considered that ladies needed help in guarding their chastity; the last two generations have passed the responsibility to the young people themselves. . . . We are putting a greater weight of responsibility on young girls to-day than they have ever had to bear in the past for their own sexual conduct." [1] There is a double caution here —first, we never have enough knowledge to pass final judgment on a person, let alone a whole generation; secondly, the formative influences on children are not confined to the home, though the home will naturally have the greatest influence of all.

But when all this has been said, we have no right to ignore what is happening in our midst. The following facts should be sufficient to awaken deep concern. Between 1958 and 1959 Church of England Moral Welfare workers dealt with an *increase* of 31% of pregnant girls under 16. The total number of girls in that age group rose by only 4%. Cases of gonorrhoea in the age group 15–19 rose by more than 65% between 1957 and 1960. The divorce rate has fallen since the peak of 58,444 in 1947, but in 1960 23,369 decrees were made absolute (petitions numbered 28,542), in 1961 24,936 (petitions 32,152).[2] At the end of 1962 there were 9,300 children in the care of the L.C.C. of whom 967 had come into care through homelessness. Local authorities, social

[1] *England in the Eighteenth Century*, Gorer, pp. 150–1, quoted by Fletcher op. cit., p. 160.
[2] Dunstan, op. cit., pp. 60, 67.

workers and wardens of homes are doing an excellent job within the limits of their powers, but, however kind the treatment they receive, children separated from their parents tend to become unstable. " Increasingly it is being found that the parents of these children are themselves the products of local authority homes and institutions. The problem is therefore to a certain extent self-perpetuating." [1]

Now we are concerned with the present and the future, not with the past; and even if it be true that to-day family life is more stable and behaviour better, or at least not worse, than in times past, we have no business to allow comparisons to lull us into self-satisfaction and complacency. " No worse than " is the tranquilliser of conscience, " better than " is the germ of pride. An excellent protection against both can be found in the translation of Galatians 6: 4 and 5 in the New English Bible, " Each man should examine his own conduct for himself; then he can measure his achievement by comparing himself with himself and not with anyone else. For everyone has his own proper burden to bear." Our burden is that we are faced with these facts at a time when so much has been done to remove the hazards to which family life was exposed. People have never been so well-off, children never more healthy and better educated, the Welfare State has done much to remove the ugly fears of sickness, unemployment and old age, the emancipation of women has made possible a richer partnership in marriage. And yet the symptoms of unstable homes are constantly before us.

There is an obvious connection between unstable

[1] *The Times* article " General Unawareness of the Fate of Homeless Children," p. 3, 28th December, 1962.

homes and unstable children. Instability may be due to one or more of many causes, some of them quite beyond the control of parents who are doing their best —sometimes heroically—in very difficult circumstances. If then we mention one particular danger, it is not because it is the only one, but because its significance is not always realised. There is a danger that we may become *a divorcing society*, as Dr. Langmead Casserley points out. This is such an important distinction and so little realised —least of all by our law-makers—that we must quote Dr. Casserley in full.

> They (the politicians and lawyers) did not understand how it is that an accepted legal enactment slowly creates a living social institution, and how a living social institution in its turn slowly creates conforming social habits and attitudes. Thus a monogamous society tolerating divorce in exceptional circumstances slowly transforms itself into a divorcing society in which monogamy is no longer a ruling social institution but a worthy and desirable religious and ethical ideal. There is a profound difference between an institution and an ideal. The institution can summon to its aid both the idealism of the idealists and also the strong tendencies toward social conformity at work in any and every society, even among non-idealists. But the ideal has nothing to rely upon except the idealism of the idealists alone.[1]

Family life is the training ground for all kinds of community life. How is community life faring to-day? It presents a very dismal picture. Take the brilliant

[1] Langmead Casserley, *The Bent World*, p. 165. See the whole chapter, "The Divorcing Society."

satire on industrial relations in the film *I'm All Right, Jack* and we can see how far off a real community spirit are the relations between employers and employed. Nowadays psychology is teaching industry many a lesson about the problems of efficiency and production and it has shown that " what counts in the long run is the mutual respect of employer and employee. The technique of teaching management how best to co-operate with labour is becoming a major preoccupation." [1] But any ordinary, decent person knows this without the aid of a psychologist. Furthermore his incentive will not be merely higher output, but his bounden duty to treat people properly, to understand them and to feel his responsibility for them. " The real and underlying desire of the worker is to be loved, and the essence of industrial management and administration is the creation of happy and harmonious working units in which the worker can discover, perhaps at first to his incredulous surprise, that he can be and is loved." [2] There is not the slightest doubt that the Welfare State is sapping the sense of responsibility and not least parental responsibility; and the reason is the failure to understand that Welfare does not simply mean material welfare and that the State ought to be a Community. This is one of the saddest pictures to-day because the Welfare State has brought untold blessings to thousands of people. But for all that we are paying a very high price, if we are becoming a people who will take all they can and give as little as they can; and more dangerous still, if under beneficent but bureaucratic controls and regulations the individual is

[1] Murdo Ewen Macdonald, *The Need to Believe*, p. 23.
[2] Langmead Casserley, *The Retreat from Christianity in the Modern World*, p. 122.

lost. It has always been the glory of this country that charitable and voluntary organisations have worked side by side with the State and Local Government. But there is a tendency to-day to crowd out these voluntary efforts whose chief function is to care for the individual. To-day people are often referred to officially as " units ", school children are drawn from " catchment areas ", a child can describe herself as a " junior mixed " and thousands of youngsters are let loose on the world as " the bulge ".

The Fatherhood of God means the Brotherhood of Man. To-day science has largely eliminated the barriers of space and time. We have more opportunity to see each other, to speak to each other and to understand each other than ever before. But what do we do with our opportunities? Apartheid in Africa, ugly race riots even in this country, a vile recrudescence of anti-Semitism and overshadowing us all the Iron and Bamboo Curtains and the gulf between East and West. But long ago St. Paul did the world the inestimable service of showing that Christianity, so far from being the new religion of a privileged race, was the good news which was to pierce every man-made curtain and barrier. Writing to Gentiles he said:

But now in union with Christ Jesus you who once were far off have been brought near by the shedding of Christ's blood. For he is himself our peace. Gentiles and Jews, he has made the two one, and in his own body of flesh and blood has broken down the enmity which stood like a dividing wall between them . . . for through him we both alike have access to the Father in the one Spirit.[1]

[1] Ephesians 2 : 13, 14, 18.

Unity, peace, the barriers of enmity broken down, access for all to the Father of all—what a contrast to the picture we have painted! But it is no use burying our heads in the sand; indeed we cannot do so if we pray the Lord's Prayer, for the first two words imply that family life is God's way of teaching us to live together in harmony. Even those who do not relate this principle to God recognise its importance and in consequence recognise the true significance of marriage as " an honourable estate . . . not by any to be enterprised, nor taken in hand, unadvisedly, lightly or wantonly . . . but duly considering the causes for which Matrimony was ordained."

The Prayer Book gives three causes which, in the 1928 Marriage Service, read as follows:

First, It was ordained for the increase of mankind according to the will of God, and that children might be brought up in the fear and nurture of the Lord, and to the praise of his holy name.

Secondly, It was ordained in order that the natural instincts and affections, implanted by God, should be hallowed and directed aright; that those who are called of God to this holy estate, should continue therein in pureness of living.

Thirdly, It was ordained for the mutual society, help, and comfort, that the one ought to have of the other, both in prosperity and adversity.

It is by no means necessary to regard these as given in order of priority.

The family is set up by a complete and, as Christianity alleges, an irrevocable giving of two persons to each

35

other for what theology calls *consortium totius vitæ*, "the sharing of the whole of life," a giving whose permanent character is manifested by the fact that the private offering and acceptance of the man and woman by each other is expressed by a public interchange of vows in the face of the social community or its representatives, and which is ultimately sealed by a physical act which is of so intimate a nature and penetrates so deeply into every recess, both physical and mental, of the personality that, according to traditional Christian doctrine, nothing within the order of nature, except the death of one of the parties, can subsequently relax the union that has been set up between them . . . they are in the biblical phrase, "one flesh". Hence, as Christian tradition teaches, indissolubility is not confined to Christian marriage, but is rooted in marriage as a natural human institution.[1]

Thus the procreation of children is not the only cause for which matrimony was ordained, and "in recent years theologians have tended strongly to the view that the mutual perfection of husband and wife is the primary reason of marriage."[2]

The same view was clearly expressed at the last Lambeth Conference.

Husbands and wives owe to each other and to the depth and stability of their families the duty to express, in sexual intercourse, the love which they bear and mean to bear to each other. Sexual inter-

[1] *The Importance of being Human*, E. L. Mascall, pp. 43, 44. See the whole chapter, "Individual and Society."
[2] op. cit., p. 46.

course is not by any means the only language of earthly love, but it is, in its full and right use, the most intimate and most revealing. . . . Therefore it is utterly wrong to urge that, unless children are specifically desired, sexual intercourse is of the nature of sin. It is also wrong to say that such intercourse ought not to be engaged in except with the willing intention to procreate children.[1]

The logical consequence of this—Family Planning and the use of contraceptives—was recognised by the same Conference.[2] The leaders of the Church have to be very, very careful before they make pronouncements which may influence our conduct and our moral standards. They can never follow popular opinion and practice merely because it is popular. This would simply lead to the dangerous spiral of directions chasing lower moral standards which is precisely the tendency followed by our law-makers to-day.[3] But in this case the bishops were merely saying what thousands of happily married people have known for a long time. The popular Press singled it out as headline news because sex is always a best-seller. But to many good-living Christians it would hardly bring any sense of relief that the bishops sanctioned what they had always practised with a perfectly clear conscience. And for once at any rate the popular conscience was sound. The bishops, of course, were influenced by the terrible population problem which confronts

[1] Lambeth Conference, 1958, Report of the Committee on " The Family in Contemporary Society," 2. p. 147.

[2] It is only fair to note that Mascall finds in his view of marriage quoted above " the most convincing argument yet urged against artificial contraception."

[3] e.g. the relaxation of the divorce and gambling laws.

the whole world—an increase of about 90,000 a day, or " a cup-tie crowd arriving in the world every day without ration books." [1] It is pertinent to ask whether this problem might be less acute if Church leaders had been more far-seeing and spoken earlier.

But when all this has been said, it is still true that the natural result of marriage is a family and that marriage is not complete until the husband-wife relationship passes into the father-mother relationship. This is the highest privilege and the greatest responsibility that human beings can accept. " Even if the essential *meaning* of marriage is the mutual union of husband and wife, the procreative end is one of transcendent splendour and dignity. For it witnesses to an almost incredible gift of God to man, namely the power to co-operate with God in the production of new human persons." [2] Thus,

> responsible parenthood implies a watchful guard against selfishness and covetousness, and an equally thoughtful awareness of the world into which our children are to be born. Couples who postpone having children until certain financial goals are reached, certain possessions gained, need to be vigilant lest they are putting their own comfort ahead of their duty. Similarly those who carelessly and improvidently bring children into the world, trusting in an unknown future or a generous society to care for them, need to make a rigorous examination of their lack of concern for their children and for the society of which they are part.[3]

[1] I cannot trace the source of this phrase.

[2] Mascall, op. cit., p. 47.

[3] Lambeth Conference, Report of the Committee on " The Family in Contemporary Society," 2. p. 146.

These considerations are all the more important because the social scene has changed and with it the pattern of marriage and family life. To-day there is a definite trend to marry at an early, sometimes at a very early, age. With this the " conception of marriage has tended to become more ' individualistic,' in that those who marry may think of their relationship as a purely private affair which has little or no relation to the families from which they come." Thus,

> a pattern of married life seems to be establishing itself which has two stages. First comes " marriage," during which stage man and wife both work outside the home. Thus the break between unmarried and married existence is less marked than commonly it used to be. It is the beginning of the second stage, when the couple " start a family," that involves the revolutionary change in their manner of life. Often this is the most critical point of personal adjustment.[1]

It is useless to ignore or to condemn out of hand changes which have obviously come to stay even if they make the achievement of real family life more difficult. Christians have to show how true marriage and family life can be achieved in spite of difficult circumstances. And this inevitably involves " family planning ", not only in the sense of deciding when and how many children shall be born, but the long and responsible duty of their up-bringing. Jesus said, " Let the little ones come to me," and that means that the home and the state, parents and law-makers, must give to children all the care and

[1] Report for the Lambeth Conference, " The Family in Contemporary Society," p. 125.

protection that love and thought and understanding can provide. Children must find in the home affection, security and significance. Or we can put this in the words we have already used—love with discipline, dependence with freedom, security with responsibility.

To-day juvenile delinquency is one of the most serious problems confronting parents and governments. Here is a circular issued to the Police Department of Houston, Texas, which is both a warning and an accusation.

FOR PARENTS

How to make a child into a Delinquent:

12 Easy Rules

1. Begin at infancy to give the child everything he wants. In this way, he will grow up to believe the world owes him a living.
2. When he picks up bad language, laugh at him. This will make him think he's cute.
3. Never give him any spiritual training. Wait until he is 21 and then let him " decide for himself."
4. Avoid the use of the word " wrong ". It may develop a guilt complex. This will condition him to believe later, when he is arrested for stealing a car, that society is against him and he is being persecuted.
5. Pick up everything he leaves lying around, books, shoes, clothes. Do everything for him so that he will be experienced in throwing all responsibility on others.
6. Let him read any printed matter he can get his hands on. Be careful that the silverware and

drinking glasses are sterilised, but let his mind feast on garbage.

7. Quarrel frequently in the presence of your children. In this way they will not be too shocked when the home is broken up later.

8. Give a child all the spending money he wants. Never let him earn his own. Why should he have things as tough as you had them?

9. Satisfy his every craving for food, drink and comfort. See that every sensual desire is gratified. Denial may lead to harmful frustration.

10. Take his part against neighbours, teachers, policemen. They are all prejudiced against your child.

11. When he gets into real trouble, apologise for yourself by saying: " I never could do anything with him."

12. Prepare for a life of grief. You will be likely to have it.

Russia has the same problem. " Everything that has ever been said in the West about broken homes and sordid environments producing juvenile delinquency applies in the Soviet Union, but on a nation-wide scale." [1] Their *stilyagi* are our beatniks; they too have sons and daughters of the well-to-do who spend their time in an entirely useless life of drinking and jiving. There is no comfort in knowing that the East faces the same problems as the West; there is, however, the discomfort of realising that we have both lost or are losing something through

[1] *Russia without Stalin*, Crankshaw, p. 122. See the whole chapter, " The Young Idea."

which alone the young can find true significance and fulfilment.

If we look back on the past century, we can be truly thankful that the awakened conscience of the nation is reflected in the enormous amount of legislation which has been directed towards the care of children. Through this " golden thread of humanity . . . our age is one of children's law—in health, in education, in factory legislation, in criminal law and the corrective training of young delinquents. If we have cause for shame over the past, we may take pride in the present for the efforts that have been made in our time, inadequate as they may be, to ensure a better future for succeeding generations." [1] They have physical and educational benefits which were non-existent fifty, let alone a hundred, years ago. But Professor Graveson uses the words " inadequate as they may be", and all these efforts *are* inadequate in two important respects. A great deal of the legislation which directly or indirectly concerns children is ambulance work, not preventive. Everyone knows that the chief sufferers from broken homes are the children. Thus one might expect legislation to be directed towards guarding the stability of home and family, and particularly by encouraging and subsidising the numerous voluntary societies which are working to this end. But what do we find? " In the three years during which £12,000 was paid by the State for Marriage Guidance, no less than £1,200,000 was paid for free and assisted legal aid, mostly for divorce cases." [2] The same writer says that " when dealing with our present laws of divorce,

[1] R. H. Graveson in *A Century of Family Law*, pp. 18, 19. Editors R. H. Graveson and F. R. Crane.

[2] *Marriage Failures and the Children*, Claud Mullins, p. 34.

the language of the stable seems suitable: such laws were by Government Neglect out of Doubtful Theology."[1]

The second way in which legislation is inadequate is the simple fact that " there is comparatively little that is fundamental that the State can do for children, for before the State has any real control over the children's lives, they can be made or marred by their parents." [2] There is not the slightest doubt that a great deal that has been won for children has been at the cost of diminished parental responsibility.

An anonymous cynic whom I have not been able to trace wrote these lines:

> Bless the clean clinic which weighed me with care
> And the Nursery School teacher who tooth-combed
> my hair,
> And the Youth Movement leader so careworn for
> me;
> But my mother, God bless her, she never sees me.

As the process of nationalising the children and emancipating their parents from responsibility for them continues, there will be less and less reason for wonder at the volume of juvenile crime, and statistics showing the numbers of divorces and neglected children will continue at a high level.[3]

The child is " fearfully and wonderfully made." [4] He is an indivisible personality, and " to the Christian the full development of personality has no meaning save with reference to the end for which he believes God has created

[1] op. cit., p. 5.　　　　[2] op. cit., p. 58.
[3] op. cit., p. 60.　　　　[4] Psalm 139 : 13.

us. . . . What in the light of this does education mean? Education is by definition, and indeed also by derivation, a feeding; the feeding of the whole indivisible personality of the human being with food that will promote his growth towards his natural end, the end for which he was born." [1] If, then, we say that God is our Father, and that every child is a child of God, there can be no question of treating religion as one subject among many. Without it education has no meaning and to deprive children of it is to starve them and stunt their natural development. Thus by far the most important parental responsibility is the religious and moral training of children. The fact that religious instruction in schools is now compulsory may lead parents to think that all that needs to be done is done at school and nothing need be done by home or Church. Thus an admirable provision and concern for at least some religious background to education may become a positive danger if it is forgotten that nothing can be a substitute for religion in the home; that state education does not touch children during the first five important years; and that religious instruction divorced from worship is sterile. Religion is more caught than taught and if parents have nothing to give, if their attitude is " don't do as I do, do as I say," then indeed their children may be physically and mentally well-nourished, but they will be deprived children.

There is one more need in home and family life which the law cannot supply—forgiveness and reconciliation. It is, of course, a separate clause in the Lord's Creed in the Lord's Prayer. But like all the other clauses it stems from " Our Father", as the branches stem from the trunk of a tree. " Many tensions in marriage and family

[1] *Christian Education Reviewed*, Spencer Leeson, p. 10.

life are allowed to reach a breaking point because self-righteousness or a sense of injury takes priority of forgiveness." [1] " The innocent party " is a popular conception which has no place in the Lord's Prayer. There are many, many husbands and wives—and children—grievously hurt, more sinned against than sinning. Every priest, every teacher, every probation officer knows this. But none of us is entirely innocent, we are all sinners. And as the Father went out to meet his son while he was a great way off and took him back to a son's place in the home, husbands and wives, fathers and mothers—and children too—have to forgive and to do all they can to mend broken homes. The greater the wrong, the wider the breach, the more need for the healing power of reconciliation and forgiveness. Only a love which is a pale reflection of our Father's love will enable us to do this.

Let us summarise briefly what we have learnt of our Lord's Creed from the first two words of the Lord's Prayer. The Creed starts with the nature of God himself. The word " Father " establishes the basic doctrine that God is Love. Then because he is *our* Father, we are all one family. From this it follows that the human family belongs to the divine ordering of the world. It is in itself a fulfilment of God's purpose of peace, concord and community life, and also the means whereby that purpose is to be extended throughout the world. Therefore marriage is a natural human institution establishing a permanent relationship, and that permanence is not confined to Christian marriage. The procreation of children is not the sole purpose of marriage, for husband and wife

[1] Lambeth Conference 1958, Resolution 116.

are already a family. But God has entrusted to us the staggering privilege and the responsibility of bringing new human beings into the world. We call these " little ones " our children, but they are also his. They can only develop into mature manhood if they are brought up to know and to love God and to find their place in his family. We who brought them into the world must bring them into the family of God.

Faced with this tremendous responsibility we shall do well to ponder, and to take courage from, these words written by St. Paul from prison:

When I think of the greatness of this great plan I fall on my knees before God the Father (from whom all fatherhood, earthly or heavenly, derives its name), and I pray that out of the glorious richness of his resources he will enable you to know the strength of the Spirit's inner reinforcement—that Christ may actually live in your hearts by your faith. And I pray that you, firmly fixed in love yourselves, may be able to grasp (with all Christians) how wide and deep and long and high is the love of Christ—and to know for yourselves that love so far from our comprehension. Now to him who by his power within us is able to do far more than we ever dare to ask or imagine—to him be glory in the Church through Jesus Christ for ever and ever, amen![1]

[1] Ephesians 3 : 14–end. (Phillips' translation.)

III. WHICH ART IN HEAVEN

God, in all that is most living and incarnate in him, is not far away
from us, altogether apart from the world we see, touch, hear, smell,
taste about us. Rather he awaits us every instant in our action, in
the work of the moment. There is a sense in which he is at the tip
of my pen, my spade, my brush, my needle—of my heart and of
my thought.

> Teilhard de Chardin, *Le Milieu Divin*, pp. 36, 37

If one would raise oneself to the eternal, it is not enough to depreciate
the temporal. . . . To raise oneself to God, it is not enough to
depreciate the world. . . . (People) believe that, because they have
not the boldness to be wordly, they are godly; not brave enough to
be on man's side, they believe they are on God's side; not belonging
to man, they think they belong to God. Because they love nobody,
they believe they love God.
And yet Jesus Christ was a man.

> Péguy, quoted by Congar in *Lay People in the Church*, p. 413

THE FIRST TWO CLAUSES in the Lord's Prayer differ
from the rest in that they are invocations, not petitions,
and these invocations tell us something about the nature
of God. The collects in our Prayer Book frequently
follow the same pattern. Thus we have " Almighty and
everlasting God, who dost govern all things in heaven and
earth " (Epiphany 2); " from whom all good things do
come " (Rogation); " Lord of all power and might "
(Trinity 7); " without whom nothing is strong, nothing
is holy " (Trinity 4); " whose never failing providence
ordereth all things in heaven and earth " (Trinity 8).

" Our Father " and " which art in heaven " are complementary, the latter asserting the transcendence, the
former the immanence of God. The transcendence
means that he is before everything, above everything,
behind everything. God is before time. " In the beginning God " remains true however far back science may
trace the origin of life and the structure of the universe.
He is above everything, and however far the astronaut
travels into space, God is still beyond him,

> Out beyond the shining
> Of the furthest star
> Thou art ever stretching
> Infinitely far.

He is beyond space and time, not as we are restricted by
the conditions of this stage of life. He is also Lord of
the universe, self-sufficient, omnipotent, omniscient.
Everything owes its origin to him. " The God who
created the world and everything in it, and who is Lord
of heaven and earth, does not live in shrines made by
men. It is not because he lacks anything that he accepts
service at men's hands, for he himself is the universal
giver of life and breath and all else. . . . In him we live
and move, in him we exist." [1] Jesus put this more simply
and more beautifully. " Are not sparrows two a penny?
Yet without your Father's leave not one of them can
fall to the ground. As for you, even the hairs of your
head have all been counted. So have no fear; you are
worth more than any number of sparrows." [2]

The words " imminent " and " immanent " are dis-
tinguished by one letter only, but the difference of meaning is profound. Both come from the Latin; the former

[1] Acts 17 : 24, 25, 27.   [2] Matthew 10 : 29–31.

means " hanging over " or even " threatening "; the
latter " flowing or trickling into". Thus immanent
exactly describes the way in which the transcendent Lord
of the universe enters into his world and into human life.
He is present in his world, always, everywhere, but he
does not force himself upon it. " Our Father " does not
directly assert the immanence of God, but it does so
implicitly, for how can a loving Father not be concerned
with everything that concerns his children? How can
he leave them to fend for themselves ? We who inherit
the Christian faith and can look back on nineteen hundred
years of Christian experience know that Jesus came to
give us this assurance and that in him we have a living
image of God immanent in the world. This truth has
been described in many ways. " When in former times
God spoke to our forefathers, he spoke in fragmentary
and varied fashion through the prophets. But in this
final age he has spoken to us in the Son . . . the Son
who is the effulgence of God's splendour and the stamp
of God's very being." [1] St. Paul says of Jesus, " the
divine nature was his from the first; yet he did not think
to snatch at equality with God, but made himself nothing,
assuming the nature of a slave. Bearing the human
likeness, revealed in human shape, he humbled himself,
and in obedience accepted even death—death on a
cross." [2] St. John writes, " He was in the world, but the
world, though it owed its being to him, did not recognise
him. He entered his own realm, and his own would not
receive him." [3]

Perhaps the simplest and most beautiful record is the
Emmaus story in which, as two men were walking along
and sharing their bitter disappointment, " Jesus himself

---

[1] Hebrews 1 : 1–3   [2] Philippians 2 : 6–8.   [3] John 1 : 10, 11.

came up and walked along with them." [1] Thus did Jesus come to reveal in his own person the eternal truth that the God of love is ever entering into his world, ever flowing into the hearts of his own people if they will receive him. The tragedy is that so many would not and will not receive him.   But " to all who did receive him, to those who have yielded him their allegiance, he gave the right to become children of God." [2]   Francis Thompson speaks for thousands when he says:

> His shoulder did I hold
> Too high that I, o'erbold
>   Weak one,
> Should lean thereon.
>
> But He a little hath
> Declined His stately path,
>   And my
> Feet set more high;
>
> That the slack arm may reach
> His shoulder, and faint speech,
>   Stir
> His unwithering hair.
>
> And bolder now and bolder
> I lean upon that shoulder,
>   So dear
> He is and near.[3]

We need to remind ourselves that these lines record the experience of many who have not *seen* Jesus.   The Ascension of Jesus did not mark the end of God's presence in the world.   It was not a desertion.   The disciples

[1] Luke 24 : 15.   [2] John 1 : 12.
[3] " Any Saint."

knew they were to *see* him no more; and yet " they returned to Jerusalem with great joy." [1] God was immanent in his world before Jesus came and he still is:

> Speak to him thou for He hears, and Spirit with
>   Spirit can meet—
> Closer is He than breathing, and nearer than hands
>   and feet.[2]

That has been the continuing experience of countless people all down the ages. Jesus " left the here that he might be everywhere." It is perfectly natural to look up " above the bright blue sky " when we think of heaven and the transcendence of God. But the disciples were warned not to forget the complementary truth of his immanence. " Men of Galilee, why stand there looking up into the sky? This Jesus, who has been taken away from you up to heaven, will come in the same way as you have seen him go."[3] " Down " and " up " are totally misleading unless we remember that they do not connote place but condition.

> The highest place that heaven affords
>   Is his, is his by right,

because " the Lord is King, be the people never so un-patient, the earth never so unquiet." [4] But soon the disciples learnt what the promise of Jesus meant. " I will not leave you bereft; I am coming back to you." [5] " I am with you always, to the end of time." [6] They realised that he never had left them, and thus for them and for us the revelation of God is complete. We know

[1] Luke 24 : 52.
[2] " The Higher Pantheism," Tennyson.
[3] Acts 1 : 11.
[4] Psalm 99 : 1.
[5] John 14 : 18.
[6] Matthew 28 : 20.

him as " our Father "; of Jesus we can say " my Lord and my God "; and the Holy Spirit, the Spirit of truth, will guide us into all truth; for, said Jesus, he " will teach you everything, and will call to mind all that I have told you," [1] " for everything that he makes known to you he will draw from what is mine." [2]

Thus we are brought face to face with the experience which the Church has done its best to guard in the doctrine of the Trinity, and the relevant words are " experience" and " done its best". The experience came first. It always does because all doctrine is based on experience. No one will claim that human language or credal formula can adequately describe the truths about God, and especially the mystery of the Triune Personality of God. To say that it is a mystery means not that it is beyond reason but beyond finite comprehension. Ultimate reality always ends in mystery. Finite beings cannot comprehend the infinite; if they could they would cease to be finite. But they can apprehend the truth in mystery. The Church " has done its best " to guard three great truths—the unity of God, the personality of God, and the experience of God in three " persons". God is one. It is essential to guard the unity of God against the idolatry of polytheism and any form of dualism which leaves the universe under two contending powers. Both alternatives are intolerable to reason and instinct. Secondly, God must be personal. This does not mean simply that God is " a person", but that he cannot be less than man who is personal. There must be within God at least the attributes of personality—reason, will and love. It is because God is personal that man can know him, love him and speak to him. We can neither

[1] John 14 : 26. [2] John 16 : 24.

know, love nor communicate with a "Life Force", a "Great First Cause" or "Fate". "In the nature of things there subsists a righteous mind and will—that is, something not less than supreme personality. . . . I cannot attach a meaning to moral values except as values for a person." [1] But this supreme personality is experienced in three ways, three "persons", Father, Son and Holy Spirit. There is the Triunity or Triune Personality of God. "This thought of God as triune was implicit—necessarily implicit—in the actual experience which the apostles had of the divine redemption through Jesus Christ; . . . as made explicit (though human language could never do justice to the reality) it did relieve the Christianised intelligence of a formidable difficulty. It did suggest how, prior to all creation, the fullness of life could be in the one God; and it found in the unfathomable depths of the divine being the ground and principle of that fellowship which is of the essence of personal life as we know it." Thus we may claim that the idea of the "triunity" of God is, "if not discoverable by reason, yet satisfying to reason," [2] content to acknowledge the mystery, but thankful that we have so much that we can understand and see and love about the transcendent-immanent God who is our Father and the Way, the Truth and Life.

These two aspects of God—his transcendence and his immanence—have to be held together, otherwise we are led into heresy; and heresy simply means to stress one aspect of the truth to the exclusion of another and complementary one. To do this with the immanence of God

---

[1] *The Philosophy of the Good Life*, Gore, p. 208.
[2] op. cit., 227–8. See the whole of Chapter IX on the "Transcendence, Immanence and Triunity of God."

leads to pantheism which means that God is in everything and everything is God. The beauty of nature
declares the glory of God, but nature is not God. We
must not confuse the Creator with his creation. We
may say, as the widow of Shunem did, " I perceive that
this is a holy man of God, who is continually passing our
way " [1]; but the man is not God. Jesus said, " Dwell
in me, as I in you," but we are the branches and he is
the vine, and " no branch can bear fruit of itself." [2] If
we will receive him to live in us, then we can " reflect
as in a mirror the splendour of the Lord; thus we are
transfigured into his likeness, from splendour to splendour." [3] The real danger of pantheism is that it removes
all moral distinctions; for if God is in everything and
everything is God, then he is the author of evil as well
as good. God tells the thief to go and steal and warns
the householder against him. In the end pantheism
robs us of our God who is the source of truth, beauty and
goodness and who cannot be the origin of anything false,
ugly and evil.

To stress the transcendence of God to the exclusion of
his immanence can be equally disastrous. This leads
to deism, a God remote from the world, uninterested in
it. He has wound up the universe like a clock and left it
to run by itself. At best, he is seen as occasionally inter-
vening in the world, a *deus ex machina* who comes to help
us sometimes, but is not with us all the time. At worst,
his sphere of influence and control becomes narrower
and narrower as knowledge increases and man gains
more mastery over nature and grows more self-sufficient
—and arrogant. If the universe is like a vast and intricate
machine, it requires a mind to work it. This is one of

[1] II Kings 4 : 9.　　[2] John 15 : 4.　　[3] II Corinthians 3 : 18.

the " proofs " of the existence of God who is the designing
mind behind it. But if man can usurp his place, and
himself control the universe, then he will neither need
God nor believe that he exists. This is the future that
some foresee and would welcome. Aldous Huxley's *Brave
New World* and *Brave New World Revisited* are prophetic
warnings that this kind of Golden Age of Man is a terrible
illusion; even more terrible is life under " Big Brother "
in George Orwell's *1984*. Dorothy Sayers described
what we may expect in the following verses which she
called " Progress ":

> The day that Nature gave is ending,
>   The hand of Man turns on the light;
> We praise thee, Progress, for defending
>   Our nerves against the dreadful night.

> As o'er each continent and island
>   The switches spread synthetic day,
> The noise of mirth is never silent,
>   Nor dies the strain of toil away.

> We thank thee that thy speed incessant
>   Provides upon this whirling ball
> No time to brood on things unpleasant—
>   No time, in fact, to think at all.

> Secure amid the soothing riot
>   Of crank and sound-track, 'plane and car,
> We shall not be condemned to quiet,
>   Nor left alone with what we are.

> By lavish and progressive measures
>   Our neighbour's wants are all relieved;
> We are not called to share his pleasures,
>   And in his grief we are not grieved.

Thy winged wheels o'erspan the oceans,
 Machining out the Standard Man,
Our food, our learning, our emotions,
 Are processed for us in the can.

All bars of colour, caste and nation
 Must yield to movies and the mike;
We need not seek communication,
 For thou dost make us all alike.

So be it! let not sleep nor slackness
 Impede thy Progress, Light sublime;
Nor ever let us glimpse the blackness
 That yawns behind the gates of Time.

But there is another danger in dismissing God from the world in which we live and relegating heaven to remoteness in time and place. It is the danger of an otherworldly religion. It was particularly prevalent in the nineteenth century when, in the face of the evils and sufferings of the Industrial Revolution, the Church cut such a sorry figure. " Pie in the sky " and the joys of heaven were held out as compensation for hell on earth and " Jerusalem the golden with milk and honey blest " for " dark satanic mills ". Thus Charles Kingsley spoke of " religion as the opiate of the people," a phrase which, to the shame of Christians, Communism has made very much its own. It is not strictly true to say that the Church was entirely blind and inactive, for there were always men and women like the Christian Socialists who awoke the conscience of the nation. But the Church as a body was terribly blind. An Archbishop of Canterbury once said to Disraeli, " I'm afraid we've lost the great towns." To which Disraeli replied, " Your Grace, you've never had them."

To-day we are suffering from this legacy of blindness and indifference, and the situation is far worse by reason of factors peculiar to the present century. We have had two world wars, we have witnessed an advance of science revolutionary in pace and scope, we live under a benevolent Welfare State and at present Western society enjoys a standard of living, and a rate of economic growth, quite unknown to most of mankind, both in the past and in other parts of the world to-day. Astronauts circle the globe and plan to reach the moon. In the eyes of the world the Church is entirely irrelevant to life, and the next step is that religion is too. Conduct is divorced from creed, and between the Church and the world there is a great gulf fixed and there are very few who can pass across it and many on both sides who do not want to. On one side, thousands are enjoying the fruits of Christianity and do not know that wherever Christianity has penetrated there is a legacy of civilising and humanitarian influences. They are offshoots of what God in Christ has brought to his world. But we cannot have Christianity without Christ. On the other side, there are " Christians " who see the Church as a cosy little clique, their religion as a round of religious observances and no more, oblivious to the duty and the need to practise their religion in the world. The result is the development of two standards of conduct; for some —and they the few—the Church and religion, if that sort of thing interests them; for others—the vast majority— the secular world with its own standards, or none at all, since for many the limits of the law and the fear of consequences are the only restraining influence. In other words, God is in heaven and has no concern for the world; and therefore I have no concern with him.

There is a reaction against this, but of course it has not yet reached the ordinary churchman, let alone " the Outsider ". " There are not two standards of Christian obligation, there are only different ways of responding to it. Just that is what now awaits rediscovery. . . . The distinction between sanctity and worldliness, or between what is sacred and what is secular, consists not in the things we are doing (' going to church ' or ' managing my business ') but in the temper and spirit which we bring to them." [1] It is commonly said that the Christian must be in the world but not of it, but this can be easily misinterpreted. It certainly cannot mean otherworldly and withdrawal from the world. Its true meaning can be found in Vidler's phrase " holy worldliness ", or Maritain's " secular sanctity ". These point to something much more difficult than worldliness or withdrawal from the world. They challenge us to involvement in the world and to finding our Christian life therein; and there is plenty of scriptural evidence for this. " Aim at peace with all men, and a holy life, for without that no one will see the Lord." [2] " The One who called you is holy; like him, be holy in all your behaviour " [3] (Phillips —" in every department of your lives ").

Therefore, my brothers, I implore you by God's mercy to offer your very selves to him: a living sacrifice, dedicated and fit for his acceptance, the worship offered by mind and heart. Adapt yourselves no longer to the pattern of this present world,

[1] *Vocation and Ministry*, Barry, 16, 17.
[2] Hebrews 12 : 14.
[3] I Peter 1 : 15.

but let your minds be remade and your whole
nature thus transformed. Then you will be able to
discern the will of God, and to know what is good,
acceptable and perfect. [1]

We are to present our " very selves " as a sacrifice, we
are to be holy " in every department of our lives "; but we
are not to be " adapted or squeezed into the pattern or
mould " of the world. We are to achieve " holy worldliness ". We shall have to discuss the word " holy " in
the next chapter. Here let it be said that originally it
had no moral connotation. Religion made a big jump
when it became linked with morality and " holy "
gained a moral significance. The danger is that to-day
the process may be reversed in the popular mind and
holiness once again be divorced from conduct. It is
not too late to redeem the situation because a higher
standard of conduct is expected of church people and
the Church is still expected " to give a lead " in moral
questions. But it is unhappily true that in the popular
conception the Church is so immersed in "religion" and
" religious practices " that it has no time for the problems
of everyday life and the gigantic issues that face the
world to-day.

Some Roman Catholics are facing the question of
holiness and saintly lives.[2] They emphasise that the
temporal conditions in which people work are the means
of sanctification. " Duties, and pious practices and
exercises are in discredit." One of them says, " I must

[1] Romans 12 : 1, 2. Phillips, " Don't let the world around you
squeeze you into its mould " is better.
[2] See *Lay People in the Church*, Yves Congar, especially Chapter VI,
and *Le Milieu Divin*, Teilhard de Chardin, pp. 36–47.

confess that I feel very embarrassed when I hear a person's Christian virtue measured solely by the criterion of his ' religious practice.' In my opinion the most important factor of all in holiness is to fulfil the duties imposed by one's state in life through love, helped and supported by a Christian community." [1] (The last words are particularly important for they are a clear condemnation of anything that turns a church into an exclusive clique, a mere collection of " the faithful ", inward-looking and complacent.) We can all think of similar embarrassments. " One of my most regular communicants "; " he has been a server for years "; " she never misses a service "; " man and boy in the choir for half a century ". All these things can be part of the training in holiness, but cannot be the sole criteria of its achievement.

A world-evading religion is a form of escapism and so to-day we have got what George MacLeod calls " the divorce between holiness and the health services." His whole book, *Only One Way Left*, is a passionate plea for holy worldliness. Vidler says, " It is a mutilated obedience (to God) which consists in being very religious and at the same time socially irresponsible." [2] And he tells of a story by Tolstoy in which a nineteenth-century duchess shed torrents of compassionate tears as she watched a melodrama on the stage whilst her coachman froze to death on the box of her carriage outside the theatre.[3] It is indeed true, as he says, that the duty of finding out what one's duty is is of all duties the most neglected.

One need is to restore to their full place and meaning the words " vocation " and " laity ". " Vocation is not

---

[1] " Worldly Holiness," Hans-Ruedi Weber in *Frontier*, January 1958, p. 22.
[2] *Christian Belief and This World*, p. 91.   [3] Vidler, op. cit., p. 102.

the exceptional prerogative of a few specially good or gifted people ('something odd that happens to a parson')," but it is the call of God to everyone. " What valid test or criterion is applicable? Perhaps the best rough-and-ready guide that can be given, in terms of human judgement, is to say that in all probability a man's vocation is what he can do best, having regard to all relevant circumstances, including his own constitutional make-up, his abilities and disabilities."[1] Thus a man's "real vocation" is the work in which he can be most useful and which he does in the belief that this is what God wants him to do. He glorifies God in his work and finds happiness in it. Similarly there are not two standards of obligation, one for the clergy, another for the laity; both are called by God to different functions in the total ministry of his Church. The laity are the Church, the people of God, and all work done in a vocational attitude is Christian work. It is a grievous mistake to equate the work of a Christian layman solely with " church work ". His work may be in office, shop, school, laboratory, industry, mine, hospital, studio or where you will; and often it is far harder for the layman to do his work as a Christian than it is for the parson.

When God is removed to a heaven remote from the world, for many people their world is without hope because it is without God.[2] But because God is in heaven, he rules the whole world and is in it. We cannot shut sanctification into a department of life, we cannot separate holiness from worldliness, devotion from duty, worship from work. The Word became flesh; he came to dwell

[1] *Vocation and Ministry*, Barry, pp. 8 and 22. On this subject see the whole of Chapter II in this valuable book.
[2] Ephesians 2 : 12.

among us. He still does. The Church is, quite literally,
the Body of Christ, the extension of the Incarnation.
Can we then doubt what our function is? How can we
achieve holiness elsewhere than where Christ walked and
talked and worked, from the carpenter's bench to the
fisherman's boat, from the wedding reception to the bed
of sickness, from the throng and press of the High Street [1]
to the fields where the sower goes forth to sow his seed?[2]
Why do we stand gazing up into the sky?

Does the fish soar to find the ocean,
The eagle plunge to find the air—
That we ask of the stars in motion
If they have rumour of thee there?

Not where the wheeling systems darken,
And our benumbed conceiving soars!—
The drift of pinions would we hearken,
Beats at our own clay-shuttered doors.

The angels keep their ancient places;—
Turn but a stone, and start a wing!
'Tis ye, 'tis your estranged faces,
That miss the many splendoured thing.

But (when so sad thou canst not sadder)
Cry;—and upon thy sore loss
Shall shine the traffic of Jacob's ladder
Pitched between heaven and Charing Cross.

[1] It is recorded that an inscription in a church was damaged by
a bomb with the result that " Glory to God in the Highest " became
" Glory to God in the High St."

[2] It should be unnecessary to add that some men and women are
called to withdrawal from the world in the "religious" life. The
validity of and the need for such vocations is not in question.

Yea, in the night, my Soul my daughter,
Cry,—clinging Heaven by the hems;
And lo, Christ walking on the water,
Not of Gennesareth, but Thames! [1]

God is in heaven, but Father Andrew quotes a French priest as saying, " We shall never find God in heaven until we find heaven in God."[2]   Heaven is to know God and be with him; and since God is present with us in the world, we can here and now find a foretaste of heaven. There is a real sense in which " God's in his heaven, all's right with the world."   " There are many dwelling-places in my Father's house," said Jesus.   " I am going there on purpose to prepare a place for you.   Where I am you may also be." [3]   The picture is of a journey with Jesus preparing the way ahead.   There is the bliss of heaven beyond this life of space and time, but life here and beyond is all one.   At every stage on the journey Jesus is there to welcome us.   Thus there is heaven all the way on the road to heaven.

It is impossible to describe heaven.   Men use the language of simile and symbol and naturally paint the sort of picture that appeals to them.   To the Jews who were not a seafaring race, there would be " no longer any sea." [4]   For the man or woman whose work is drudgery, there will be unbroken rest.   For those who know famine and hunger, there will be food in plenty.   Many of these ideas are very materialistic because here and now we are so dependent on physical conditions that we find it almost impossible to conceive of life without them.   Thus

[1] " The Kingdom of God," Francis Thompson.
[2] *The Pattern Prayer*, p. 24.   [3] John 14 : 2, 3.
[4] Revelations 21 : 1.

many of the " messages " which come from " the other side " to those who indulge in spiritism are strikingly earthbound and unattractive. But the New Testament is our sufficient guide. " Now at last God has his dwelling among men! He will dwell among them and they shall be his people, and God himself will be with them. He will wipe away every tear from their eyes; and there shall be an end to death, and to mourning and crying and pain; for the old order has passed away!"[1] There will be peace, for " on either side of the river stood a tree of life. . . . The leaves of the tree serve for the healing of the nations." [2] " The gates of the city shall never be shut by day—and there will be no night. The wealth and splendour of the nations shall be brought into it; but nothing unclean shall enter." [3] And if for some of us endless rest would mean, not simply relief from drudgery and pain, but the boredom of perpetual inactivity, we can remember the words of Jesus which paint a very different picture: " Well done, my good and trusty servant! You have proved trustworthy in a small way; I will now put you in charge of something big. Come and share your master's delight." [4] Nor must we dismiss materialistic ideas about heaven as worthless. There is a very important truth in them. John saw " a new heaven and a new earth " and he heard a voice saying, " Behold! I am making all things new." [5] St. Paul wrote, " The universe itself is to be released from the shackles of mortality and enter upon the liberty and splendour of the children of God." [6] Thus in some stupendous and mysterious way the whole created universe

[1] Revelation 21 : 3, 4. [2] Revelation 22 : 2.
[3] Revelation 21 : 25–7. [4] Matthew 25 : 21.
[5] Revelation 21 : 1, 5. [6] Romans 8 : 21.

will be redeemed and built into the City of God. In heaven we shall " have our perfect consummation and bliss, both in body and soul." [1] Nothing that makes life happy and sweet and useful will be lost. The source of all life is " in the beginning God " [2] and in the end " God will be all in all." [3]

God will be all in all, nothing will be lost. And no one? Father Andrew dares to say " Heaven is only heaven to us because God is there, and, though it may baffle our reason, in a sense heaven is not heaven to him if we are not there." [4] The shepherd is not content with ninety-nine sheep; he *must* go to seek even one which has lost its way. Or, to recall the divine principle of home and family life, just as the human family is incomplete where there is an empty chair, so our Father must have his whole family around him in heaven. Is there then no hell? We must at least be consistent. We have spoken of a foretaste of heaven here and now. If heaven is to know God and to receive him into our lives, to refuse him and to live without him must be hell. So would Marlowe have us understand:

Faustus

Where are you damned?

Mephistophilis

In Hell.

Faustus

How comes it then that thou art out of Hell?

---

[1] Book of Common Prayer, " At the Burial of the Dead."
[2] Genesis 1 : 1.
[3] I Corinthians 15 : 28.
[4] *The Pattern Prayer*, Father Andrew, p. 32.

Mephistophilis
Why this is Hell, nor am I out of it:
Think'st thou that I who saw the face of God,
And tasted the eternal joys of Heaven,
Am not tormented with ten thousand Hells,
In being deprived of everlasting bliss? [1]

But the deprivation is by our own choice. God is always knocking at the door of our lives,[2] but there is no handle on the outside. We have to open it. In the parable [3] the younger son left home for a distant country. For a time he enjoyed himself. But there came a famine and no one gave him anything. Men make their own hell when they leave their Father's home; and in an affluent society they suffer " not a famine of bread, nor a thirst for water, but a famine of hearing the words of the Lord." [4] The result may be spiritual atrophy, for the natural law obtains in the spiritual world. The mole spends its life burrowing beneath the ground; nature has closed up its eyes. The hermit-crab takes up its abode in the shell of another animal; it has lost the thick shell which used to cover the abdominal region of its body.[5] This is the meaning of the parable of the talents. " The man who has not will forfeit even what he has." [6] The son came to his senses in time and returned home. Some do not even know there is home to go to. They are lost.

For ever? Can heaven be heaven if God's family is

---

[1] *The Tragical History of Dr. Faustus.*   [2] Revelation 3 : 20.
[3] Luke 15 : 15 ff.   [4] Amos 8 : 11.
[5] See an old but interesting book, *Natural Law in the Spiritual World*, H. Drummond.
[6] Matthew 25 : 29.

not complete? Can we say that *in the end* God's infinite
love will win all men to him? Jesus said, " I shall draw
all men to myself, when I am lifted up from the earth." [1]
He was referring to his death on the Cross, not to his
ascension into heaven. The word is " draw ", not
" force "; and it must mean that all men will turn to
him of their own volition. It is the Cross too which makes
it impossible so to debase the love of God that he becomes
" the good fellow and 'twill all be well." That is the
blasphemous presumption of *Dieu pardonnera; c'est son
métier*.[2]

We have to hold together two great truths which at
first sight, as is often the case with Christian doctrine,
seem to be mutually exclusive. These truths are man's
freedom to choose and God's invincible love. " The one
says: ' Christ is all in all, and always will be '; the other
says, ' Christ has to be *chosen*, and always must be '." [3]
Man's freedom to choose must be real, for without
freedom there can be no love. No one can be sent to
hell; we can only choose it. C. S. Lewis in *The Great
Divorce* tells how the inhabitants of hell are given the
chance to visit heaven. When they get there they
cannot stand it. The grass feels like iron under their
feet, the light is unbearable, and all they ask is to go
back to hell which they have chosen. Every reference
to the New Testament emphasises the seriousness of this
choice. But the mistake comes when " infinite seriousness
is translated as endless time. And so we end with the
familiar picture of heaven and hell as two objective

[1] John 12 : 32.
[2] *In the end God. . . .*, J. A. T. Robinson, p. 120. In what follows
I have drawn considerably from this book.
[3] op. cit., p. 119.

realities finally and everlastingly co-existent side by side in God's universe. . . . We must envisage the most terrible defeat of the love of God." [1]

There is, however, one parable in the New Testament which seems not only to point to infinite seriousness, but to man's choice being limited to this life on earth. In the parable of Dives and Lazarus [2] " there is a great chasm fixed between us; no one from our side who wants to reach you can cross it, and none may pass from your side to us." Are we to assume, then, that Dives is lost for ever? We can only do so if we take this parable in isolation from the revelation of God's love in the life and death of Jesus. Generally speaking, in each parable Jesus emphasises one great truth, and here once again is the seriousness of choice. Dives is in hell because in his life on earth he had not learnt " that the man who does not love is still in the realm of death. . . . If a man has enough to live on, and yet when he sees his brother in need shuts up his heart against him, how can it be said that the divine love dwells in him? " [3] But we cannot say that he will never learn, never be drawn by that divine love which can bridge every chasm. Indeed, is there not already a glimmer of hope when his first cry " take pity on me! " becomes an appeal to send Lazarus to warn his five brothers " so that they too may not come to this place of torment "? The New Testament " never dogmatises to the extent of saying that after death there

---

[1] op. cit., pp. 121–2. Dr. Robinson rightly warns us that we can base nothing on the fact that " eternal " in the New Testament does not necessarily mean " everlasting " but enduring for an indefinitely long period. For in Matthew 25 : 46 we must give the same meaning to the word in " eternal punishment " and " eternal life".

[2] Luke 16 : 19 ff.   [3] I John 3 : 14, 17.

is no further chance. . . . No Being who had an *infinite* concern for the salvation of every soul could possibly be conceived as saying in effect: ' Unless you turn to me by the age of seventy, or seven, or seven weeks (whatever it may be), I cannot give you a further chance.' A God like that is either at the mercy of death, or he is not the God of the parable of the Prodigal." [1] Furthermore, unless we confine Christ's preaching to the dead (I Peter 4 : 6) to a single event, we may see in this the truth that " no place or time or state can possibly frustrate the purpose of God in bringing all men ultimately to the point of decision for him." [2] And to yield is not to lose freedom, but to find it. It is a willing surrender to him whose heaven is not heaven without us, for God remains on the Cross as long as one sinner remains in hell. In the end no man can endure this, in the end God will be all in all.

Have we read too much into these four words " which art in heaven "? Not if we allow that all the clauses in the Lord's Prayer are so profound that we can dig deep into their meaning to discover the doctrines implicit in them. In this clause we have been led to consider the nature of God, his transcendence, his immanence, and our experience of him in his Triune Personality. But since doctrine must govern conduct, we have discussed the dangers of an otherworldly religion or of life in the world no longer governed by God but by man. The doctrine of the Incarnation gives the lie to both these and the Church as the Body of Christ exists to carry on the work of God in the world. We then turned to consider what heaven means for us, and we could not do this

[1] Robinson, op. cit., p. 33.   [2] op. cit., p. 33, note.

without considering the meaning of hell. This brought us face to face with two great truths—man's freedom to choose and God's almighty love. The Cross of Christ can never allow us either to minimise the seriousness of choice or to think that divine love can ever condone evil. We were driven to say that in the end the crucifixion of the God of love will be unendurable and we dared to say that in the end God will draw all men to himself.

IV. HALLOWED BE THY NAME

The name Jesus contains within itself the whole of humanity and the whole of God.

> Dietrich Bonhoeffer, *Ethics*, pp. 10, 11

It is always the temptation of religious people to worship religion instead of worshipping God.

> F. R. Barry, *Vocation and Ministry*, p. 13

Plato deemed the unconscious "lie in the soul", that inability to recognise the good and the true which misleads the man himself, worse than the conscious verbal lie which is meant to mislead others. Truly a hard saying ; but Christ and Plato here seem to concur that, not sins committed, but false values and ideals are the worst peril of the soul.

> B. H. Streeter, *The Spirit*, p. 364

We live in a time when men neither love nor seek the truth. In ever greater measure, truth is being replaced by the will to power, by what is useful or valuable to special interests.

> Nicolas Berdyaev, *The Realm of Spirit and the Realm of Cæsar*, p. 13

Must then a Christ perish in torment in every age to save those that have no imagination?

> Bernard Shaw, *St. Joan*

"THE MAGIC OF A NAME." To primitive people this was literally true. They thought that a god or demon must come when his name was called. They also believed that to know a person's name gave one power over him; hence they were reluctant to give their name to a stranger. No doubt some relics of these ideas may lie behind the use of the word in the Old Testament, but the chief connection with them is that the Hebrews used

71

" name " as almost equivalent to the personality or character of the person or thing named. In the Old Testament we also read of a person's name being called over something, signifying that it came under the authority or into the possession of that person. Joab begged David to be present when the city of Rabbah fell lest his own name, and not David's, should be called over it.[1] Women have the name of their husbands called over them in marriage and thus come under their authority and protection. But the really significant thing about the Hebrews is that they substituted for the name " Jehovah " the word " Lord ", not because of fear of any magical consequence, but because they shrank from pronouncing a name so sacred. The corollary of this was that " he who blasphemes the name of the Lord shall be put to death." [2]

These three ideas—character, authority, reverence—are clearly seen in the New Testament. When Mary said " his name is holy," [3] she meant that this was the nature and character of God. When Jesus said, " I have made thy name known to the men whom thou didst give me out of the world," [4] he meant that he himself had revealed God to them. The first petition in the prayer he gave his disciples was to reverence the nature and character of God which he " named " in the first two clauses. The second idea is implied in " believers will cast out devils in my name " [5]; they would be acting with his authority and by faith in his power. For had he not said " he who has faith in me will do what I am doing; and he will do greater things still because I am

---

[1] II Samuel 12 : 28.
[2] Leviticus 24 : 16.
[3] Luke 1 : 49.
[4] John 17 : 6.
[5] Mark 16 : 17.

going to the Father "? [1] In every appeal to God they
were taught to invoke the name of Jesus, just as we end
our prayers "through Jesus Christ our Lord". No
doubt some could think that this was a kind of magical
formula. Probably the rulers had this in mind when they
asked Peter and John " by what power or by what name"
they had healed the cripple. But although Peter used
the same phrase and replied " by the name of Jesus
Christ," he certainly did not mean what they meant.[2]
Jesus had indeed said, " If you ask the Father for anything in my name, he will give it you." [3] But he himself
had prayed " in anguish of spirit " and said, " Not my
will but thine be done." [4] The disciples knew that the
prayer of faith in the power of Jesus would always be
answered, but that every prayer must be consistent with
the will of God as he himself had expressed it in his life
and teaching.

In the New Testament no less than in the Old there is
reverence for " the name". " ' Master, which is the greatest
commandment in the Law? ' He answered, ' Love the
Lord your God with all your heart, with all your soul,
with all your mind.' That is the greatest commandment.
It comes first." [5] Then when they could say to Jesus
" My Lord and my God," [6] " Jesus " became " the name
above all names, the name at which every knee should
bow." [7] They even rejoiced " that they had been found
worthy to suffer indignity for the sake of the Name." [8]
The Hebrews shrank from saying " Jehovah", but no
one shrinks from saying " Jesus ": this alone shows that

---

[1] John 14 : 12. [2] Acts 4 : 7, 10.
[3] John 16 : 23. [4] Luke 22 : 44, 42.
[5] Matthew 22 : 36–8. [6] John 20 : 28.
[7] Philippians 2 : 10. [8] Acts 5 : 41.

there is a whole world of difference between B.C. and A.D. It is not a difference of reverence, but the difference that Christ has made. Now we say "How sweet the name of Jesus sounds," "Jesu, lover of my soul," "All hail the power of Jesu's name."

> Dear name! the rock on which I build,
> My shield and hiding place,
> My never-failing treasury filled
> With boundless stores of grace.
> And may the music of thy name
> Refresh my soul in death.

Thus in "Jesus" we find all three ideas associated with "name": character, authority, reverence. And no wonder when we see "the glory of God in the face of Jesus Christ." [1]

But even that is not the whole story. There is a further reason why the name "Jesus" is precious—he came not only to reveal the nature of God, but also the true nature of man. He is MAN, not just a man. We are made in the image of God, we come from the Royal Mint and the King's likeness is stamped upon us. The image may be blurred and marred, but it is never, never lost, and as coinage of the realm we can never lose our intrinsic value. We should have done, had not Jesus come to restore the image, to redeem human nature. "You shall give him the name Jesus (Saviour), for he will save his people from their sins." [2] Thus the name "Jesus" not only inspires reverence for God, but self-reverence and reverence for all men. For if "God loved the world so much that he gave his only Son," [3] we have a right to respect ourselves

---

[1] II Corinthians 4 : 6.   [3] John 3 : 16.
[2] Matthew 1 : 21.

and a duty to respect others. " The name Jesus contains within itself the whole of humanity and the whole of God." [1]

There is a simple test of this that anyone can make. Try to cut out of your vocabulary the word " Jesus". At once the whole of the New Testament goes, and with it all the lovely stories that for ages we have taken delight in telling our children—the Good Shepherd, the Good Samaritan, the Prodigal Son. We shall lose many of our well-known hymns, and Christmas carols too, for there will be no Christmas, no Good Friday, no Easter Day. Gone too is the Cross, and its use as a symbol of valour and sacrifice will be meaningless. For why a Cross if Jesus never lived and never died? We shall no longer pray " through Jesus Christ our Lord ". The name " Christian " will have no meaning if there was no Christ. And so we might echo that bitter cry, " They have taken my Lord away, and I do not know where they have laid him." [2] But enough of this; it is intolerable. Jesus lived and lives, and " I am convinced that there is nothing in death or life . . . in the world as it is or the world as it shall be, in the forces of the universe, in heights or depths—nothing in all creation than can separate us from the love of God in Christ Jesus our Lord." [3]

The word " hallow " is not often used except in poetry and hymns and in a rather " churchy " connotation. It probably comes from the same root as " holy ", about which we have already said a good deal in connection with " holy worldliness ". We must give to " hallow " the same wide significance and rescue it from the same

[1] *Ethics*, Bonhoeffer, pp. 10, 11.
[2] John 20 : 13.   [3] Romans 8 : 38, 39.

75

danger of otherworldliness. Many will agree with
Coleridge that

> 'Tis sweet to him who all the week
> Through city-crowds must push his way,
> To stroll alone through fields and woods,
> And hallow thus the Sabbath-day.[1]

But the hard fact remains that it is precisely " all the
week " amidst the " city crowds " that our minds must
" be set to hallow all we find,"

> Room to deny ourselves, a road
> To bring us daily nearer God.[2]

And the important words are in the last line. In his
speech at the dedication of the National Cemetery at
Gettysburg, Lincoln said, " We cannot hallow this
ground "; it was hallowed already by the courage and
sacrifice of the living and the dead. Bacon said, " The
place of justice is a hallowed place." [3] Thus to hallow
God's name is to honour, respect, reverence all that the
name of God stands for, " all that is true, all that is
noble, all that is just and pure, all that is lovable and
gracious, whatever is excellent and admirable." [4]

" What is the chief end of man? " asks the Shorter
Catechism, and the answer is " To glorify God and to
enjoy him for ever." Worship is a necessity for man;
like all instincts it cries out for fulfilment and like all
other instincts it is extremely dangerous if it finds its
fulfilment in an unworthy or degraded end. People
who wish to wield power or to make money know how
to exploit this instinct. They will provide an object of

---

[1] " Home Sick."   [2] Keble, *Hymns Ancient and Modern,* 4.
[3] " Of Judicature."   [4] Philippians 4 : 8.

worship, an idol, a Hitler or a Lenin, a film star, a crooner or a professional sportsman. There is always a long queue in Moscow waiting to enter when the mausoleum where Lenin lies is open to the public. The commonest idol is oneself. We have heard the gibe, " a self-made man worships his maker." Self-worship is fantasy and like all fantasy highly dangerous because it lives on unreality. The object of man's worship must be superior to himself. If he worships a crooner, he is admitting that the crooner is superior to his poor little self. If he worships God, it means that his estimate of himself is such that nothing but the highest can satisfy him. For God is the ultimate reality, the source of all true values, and therefore to worship God is to reject false values and to acknowledge that all truth, beauty and goodness come from him.

The Christian way of life is before all things the way of worship. Power to worship is God's greatest gift to man. It is that which, more than anything else, distinguishes him from the lower creation. In worship he offers his highest to the highest that he knows. . . . What then is worship? It is the recognition of the " worth " of God. The whole of man's life may and should be its expression. But, if it is to be so, there must be " acts of worship " in which we consciously direct our minds and wills and hearts to God. Without that we run the risk of losing our sense of personal relationship with him. . . . Common worship needs to have an element of " formality ". The deepest things of life can only be so expressed. For instance, friendship with others, though a deep spiritual experience, needs to be expressed and maintained by formalities of etiquette and hospitality. We do not invite our friends to a meal merely in order to provide them with physical nourishment, but because the ritual of eating and drinking with them is a vehicle and expression of a personal relationship. A lover says to his beloved " I love you," not because he desires to convey information, but because such formal expression is a need of his soul. So the Christian's aspirations after God express themselves in the words and actions of the liturgy of the Church.[1]

William Temple once said, " This world can be saved from political chaos and collapse by one thing only and that is worship." He defined worship in these words: " To worship is to quicken the conscience by the holiness of God, to feed the mind with the truth of God, to purge the imagination by the beauty of God, to open the heart to the love of God, to devote the will to the purpose of God," and he went on to say that prayer " is one part of worship, and is in place only in that setting. That is why the first clause in the model prayer is ' Hallowed be thy name '." [2]

There are many who say they feel no need to worship or at any rate no need to worship in church. They usually claim to worship better in the open air. " The heavens declare the glory of God," and

> Earth's crammed with heaven,
> And every common bush afire with God;
> But only he who sees, takes off his shoes,
> The rest sit round it and pluck blackberries,

[1] Lambeth Conference Report, 1948, Part II, p. 29 ff.
[2] *The Hope of a New World*, pp. 26, 27, 30.

And daub their natural faces unaware
More and more from the first similitude.[1]

The truth is, not that some people have no need to
worship, but that the need is universal and everyone
worships someone or something; and if it is not God, it
is a substitute, an idol. An American writer gives some
modern equivalents of the " calf in Horeb ". " What
shape is your idol, sister? Is it your house, or your
clothes, or perhaps even your worthwhile cultural club?
I worship the pictures I paint, brother. . . . I worship
my job; I'm the best darn publicity expert this side of
Hollywood. . . . I worship my comfort; after all isn't
enjoyment the goal of life? . . . I worship my church;
I want to tell you, the work we've done for missions beats
all other denominations in the city, and next year we can
afford that new organ, and you won't find a better choir
anywhere. . . . I worship myself . . . what shape is *your*
idol? "[2]

Men must worship something and if it is not God it
will be an idol, and idolatry is not only highly dangerous,
it will not satisfy our primary need. God must come
first, and to catch some glimpse of the holiness, truth,
beauty, love and purpose of God and then in some measure
to reflect what we have found and seen is the only way
in which we shall be equipped for hallowing the name of
God in the world. For it is no easy task to hallow the
things of God in the world, and there are some very
subtle forms of idolatry. We may well ask ourselves,
" What shape is my idol? "

There is the person meticulous in pious practices,

---

[1] " Aurora Leigh," Elizabeth Barratt Browning.
[2] *Smoke on the Mountain*, Joy Davidman, p. 31.

very regular at services, who neglects his home, is careless about his children, utterly unimaginative about the refugees. There is the " Sanctuary Sammy " whose knowledge of ceremonial and ecclesiastical haberdashery is impeccable. He can put the new vicar and visiting clergy right on every detail of ceremonial, but his membership of the Body of Christ ends when he doffs his cotta or alb. It is possible to become so devoted to a cause that we entirely forget the more excellent way, charity, or be so obsessed with it that we actually turn means into ends. Thus we become fanatics and fanaticism has been defined as unlimited devotion to limited ends.

> Some men have been so devoted to a cause—one which indeed they may have taken up originally out of a real compassion for their fellow-creatures—or they may have become so egotistically attached to their own plan of salvation for the human race— that they have been ready to ride over men's broken bodies to secure their purposes. And in any case some people who work for human causes do not realise how much they may be moved by their hatreds rather than their loves—how much they really hate Germany rather than they love England, or envy the capitalist more than they actually care for the poor.[1]

And if we think that this cap fits the Communists, we shall do well to ponder what a wise man said, " There is one thing more dangerous than Communism, and that is anti-Communism." He was obviously thinking of those whose opposition springs from hatred and is purely negative. Tolstoy said, " Where love is God is." The

[1] *History and Human Relations*, Butterfield, pp. 45, 46.

converse is equally true; hatred replaces God by an idol.

There are others who are impervious to new revelations of the truth or at least suspicious of the quarters from which they came. Somewhere is recorded the story of the divine who, at the time of the Darwinian controversy, thus prayed: " O Lord, grant that this theory of evolution be not true. But if it be true, grant that it be hushed up." [1] It is a great pity when religious people sometimes give the impression that they are afraid of the advance of knowledge, especially of scientific knowledge, because it may disturb their traditional beliefs. There is something craven about this attitude, and it forgets that God is a God of truth. Truth should never disturb faith; it should confirm it by leading us to a wider and more splendid vision of God. " The whole universe, star and atom, is sacramental. Its study and its control are therefore true vocations. Perhaps the Church has not always seen this clearly enough, and by failing to provide a true critique of events, has also failed to provide the criteria by which man's science may be judged." [2]

There is also an idolatry of the Church itself, if men are impervious to goodness when it comes from outside the Church. It is sometimes said that there is more charity and goodness, more sensitiveness to injustice, more prophetic insight and search for truth outside than within the Church. That is not true. What is true is that there is a great deal of goodness, charity, justice and prophecy in the world outside the Church and that it is not always recognised for what it is. This failure means that we are substituting the Church itself for Christ,

[1] I cannot trace the source of this.
[2] *Some Problems of the Atomic Age*, C. A. Coulson, p. 22.

that we are making him the prisoner of his Church and that we are forgetting that every spark of goodness, every ray of beauty and every facet of the truth comes from " the real light which enlightens every man." [1] It makes no difference that many a man who reflects the light does not know or does not admit the source from which it comes. There is all the more need for those who profess and call themselves Christians to show these people that they are not far from the Kingdom of God, and, if we are honest, perhaps nearer than we may be ourselves. If we think and behave otherwise, we are probably very near to idolatry and very near to the " holier than thou " attitude of the Pharisee. It is only a short step from blindness to the good in others to thanking God that we are not like the rest of men.[2] " The golden rule in the Church of God is always to reverence and value the vocations of other people." [3]

Puritanism is a kind of idolatry. " Puritan society, especially when once the fires of living faith have departed, and where only the habitual puritan way of life survives—once, that is, puritanism has become no more than a drab morality without religion—easily degenerates into this depressing cult of respectability. . . . Puritanism is predominantly a lay religion, and lay religion is particularly inclined to identify its spiritual ideals with its everyday social habits and objectives." [4] There is a big difference between the puritan and the ascetic. The puritan is suspicious of all pleasure; thus he sees evil in so much that is good. The ascetic sees and reverences the good things of life; but sometimes he has to forgo some-

[1] John 1 : 9. [2] Luke 18 : 11.
[3] *Christian Community*, Langmead Casserley, p. 99.
[4] *The Bent World*, Langmead Casserley, p. 191.

thing that is good and noble, e.g. marriage, for something which, in his particular circumstances, is better and nobler still. There is a Jewish saying that " a man will have to give account on the judgment day of every good thing which he has refused to enjoy when he might have done so." [1] The puritan runs into the danger of prac- tising morality without religion, and that is morality without God. Ultimately this may become the idol of respectability and respectability can hide a multitude of sins.

Akin to this is scrupulosity. "Your trouble comes," said Francis de Sales " from fearing vices more than you love virtues." What is the remedy? " After the Grace of God it is not to be so scrupulous." On another occa- sion he said, " Mon Dieu, my daughter, I could wish that the skin of your heart were a little thicker so that you were not kept from sleeping by fleas. . . . Keep your heart spacious." [2] And Mounier adds, " spacious; in other words, to the scale of God." There is an echo of this in the title of one of J. B. Phillips's books, *Your God is Too Small*. We can so very easily in our anxieties and worries reduce God to the limits of our own myopia.

There is a scathing description of idolatry in the Psalms: " They made a calf in Horeb, and worshipped the molten image. Thus they turned their glory into the similitude of a calf that eateth hay." [3] The ultimate result of idolatry is atheism. That comes when there is not even a substitute for God, when leanness enters into

---

[1] *The Vision of God*, K. E. Kirk, p. 61, quoted by Vidler in *Essays in Liberality*, p. 99.
[2] Quoted in *The Spoil of the Violent*, Emmanuel Mounier, pp. 53, 54.
[3] Psalm 106 : 19, 20.

a man's soul [1] and " he does not abhor anything that is evil." [2] It is, in fact, nihilism.

> Nothing interesting to do
> Nothing interesting to say
> Nothing remarkable in any way:
> Then the journey home again
> In the hot suburban train
> To the tawdry new estate,
> Crumpled, grubby, dazed and late
> Home to supper and to bed
> Shall we be like this when we are dead? [3]

We are all idolaters in some way or other and some of the time; but, thank God, not all the time. When we catch a glimpse of reality, we see our idols for what they are, substitutes, poor little things. And as we learn more and more to hallow the name of God, our vision of him grows wider and we begin to see in the world so much on which he has written his name.

> Something interesting to do,
> Something interesting to say,
> Something remarkable in every way.
> When we journey home again
> In the hot suburban train,
> Back again to the new estate
> For new discoveries never too late.
> Home, supper, and comfortable bed,
> Wife, children, and nothing to dread;
> Food for body and food for mind,
> Surrounded by friends and neighbours kind.

---

[1] Psalm 106 : 15.   [2] Psalm 36 : 4.

[3] " The Ascent of F 6," Auden and Isherwood, quoted in *Watchman, What of the Night ?*, Garbett, p. 15.

Sorrows and joys and work and play
Alive to meet them each new day.
Alive to hallow in all I see
God's name on all humanity,
Writ large by Jesus on every man,
On all things lovely since life began.
I may be grubby and dazed and late,
But I've found my glorious New Estate.

To love and reverence God is the first Commandment, the second to love and respect our neighbour as ourself. And the reason is that God's name is written on all humanity. There is a very close connection here with reverence for truth, beauty and goodness. They have always been recognised as ideals and as ultimate realities, for the human mind does not create them. Furthermore, all religions hold that they presuppose a personal Spirit of truth, beauty and goodness. In other words, they are personal values having their source in a personal God. From the human standpoint they are personal too. They cannot be entirely separated, for what is good must be true and beautiful, and what is bad must be false and ugly. Philosophers and scientists may pursue truth for its own sake, and, more obviously, the artist beauty. In this sense truth and beauty may be impersonal. But clearly goodness must always be personal; moral values have no meaning except as values for a person. And since these three values are so closely inter-related, they will all reach their fulfilment as personal values. God has written his name on all that makes human life true and beautiful and good.[1]

[1] See Gore's *Philosophy of the Good Life*, especially p. 29 and Chapter VIII.

This is the clue to the Christian doctrine of man, this is what Jesus meant when he said, " I have come that men may have life, and may have it in all its fullness." [1] There is not the slightest doubt that this doctrine is especially relevant to the world's need to-day. It was the main theme of the Lambeth Conference of 1948 and the need is just as urgent to-day as it was then.[2] All problems and questions run back into this. For what is the use of discussing a planned society until we have decided what society is for, and this turns upon the nature and destiny of man. If man is to find life in all its fullness, he must not only seek what is good, beautiful and true, he must be surrounded by everything that encourages these values and he must declare war against evil, ugliness and falsehood. This necessity, which is also a duty, is expressed in the following prayer which is a commentary on " hallowed be thy name ":

Loving and Holy Spirit of God, we pray:—
That we and all men may increasingly work together to establish the kingdom of heaven upon earth;
That the resources of the earth may be gathered, distributed and used, with unselfish motives and scientific skill for the greatest benefit of all;
That beauty may be given to our towns, and left to our countryside;
That children may be finely bred and finely trained;
That there may be open ways, and peace, and freedom from end to end of the earth." [3]

[1] John 10 : 10.
[2] See the Report, part II, p. 2.
[3] *An Anthology of Prayers*, A. S. T. Fisher, p. 53.

The famous passage in the *Republic* and the *Laws*, in which Plato emphasises the supreme importance of the education of children, before they are of an age to appreciate rational processes, is based quite frankly on the idea that they should go out into the maturer stage of life with one supreme prejudice . . . that there are divine principles which must not be violated. . . . The most important period in the education of the soul is the pre-rational, the education of children to love and to hate the right things. The training of children . . . is to train the soul to love order and beauty and to *feel* aright, so that later, when the period of conscious reason comes, they can, by a sound prejudice, distinguish truth from error and right from wrong.[1]

But to-day by no means everyone would agree with Plato. We are told that there must be a new morality and that there are no moral absolutes. No doubt this is partly due to a revolt against the standards of former generations and a suspicion that a veneer of respectability covered a good deal that was wrong. There is some truth in this. But it is an excuse for, and not the cause of, the so-called new morality. Unhappily this attitude is encouraged by intelligent and well-meaning people who think aloud and in public on radio and television before a vast mixed audience, and discuss ideas which are only half-formulated and pose questions to which they give no clear answer. The result is encouragement to sceptics, discouragement to believers and bewilderment to many. Not that we should be afraid to face and discuss doubts and difficulties. Only in this way can we meet

[1] Gore, op cit., 287, 8 and 112.

honest agnosticism and unbelief and hammer out the truth. But, as Erasmus said, there are many things which may be discussed in the study which should not be noised abroad in the market-place.

Fundamentally the rejection of moral absolutes is the rejection of the absolute authority of God. It is to fly in the face of the experience of the ages that there is an impressive unanimity, not only as to what makes the Good Life for man, but also in the conviction that the values on which that Good Life is based are personal values which have their source and authority in a personal God. It is equally a matter of experience that when there are no moral absolutes, morality is at the mercy of change and decay and becomes a purely private affair. But God has written his name, not only on the individual, but on the individual in community: not because the community is more important than the individual, but because self-awareness and fullness of life can only be found in communion with God and our fellow men. There is no greater need to-day than to reassert by conviction and by example the duty, indeed the necessity, of reverencing the absolute values which bear the hallmark of the divine name.

The Christian doctrine of man asserts the sanctity of each human personality. He must never become the pawn of any system, however benevolent it may be. This is why Communism, or any form of statism, under which people become mere progress fodder, stands condemned. But it can happen here. Read Aldous Huxley's *Brave New World Revisited* and see how his former prophecies are being alarmingly fulfilled. "Never have so many been manipulated so much by so few." [1] "The beauty

[1] p. 34.

of tidiness is used as a justification for despotism." [1]
" Thanks to modern methods of communication, it is
possible to mechanise the lower leadership. As a result
of this there has arisen the new type of the uncritical
recipient of orders." [2] The political scene is dismal;
political parties give the impression that they are more
concerned with party than with people, and there is a
dearth of real leadership. There is grave danger of man
being depersonalised by mass treatment, regulations,
planning and controls. Countries spend vast sums of
money on space-research and plan to set foot on Mars or
the moon whilst millions of people are starving and
thousands of refugees have no place on earth. Cancer
takes an increasing toll of lives and the fight against it is
crippled for lack of money. And all the time we live in
peril of destroying ourselves by the misuse of God's gift
of nuclear power.

We have already spoken about home and family life,
but there is one aspect of it which is relevant in the
present context. How can there be a home without a
house? At the beginning of 1963 in the L.C.C. area
there were over 4,000 people homeless, literally homeless,
not just living in slums. As for the overall housing situation, it is shameful how little is known about it except by
the people who live in appalling conditions or cannot
find anywhere at all to live. " We are building fewer
houses in proportion to population than Germany,
Sweden, Holland, Norway and France." [3] Where is
reverence for beauty in tolerating slums, where respect

[1] p. 38.　　　[2] p. 61.
[3] *Britain in the Sixties:* 'Housing,' Stanley Alderson, p. 40. A
Penguin special giving a detailed and critical survey of Britain's
Housing to-day.

for God's children when young couples may be turned out of lodgings if they have a baby, where regard for truth in ignorance of the situation? Ignorance where human lives are concerned breeds indifference and indifference cruelty.

" Must then a Christ perish in torment in every age to save those who have no imagination? " These words are said in the epilogue of Bernard Shaw's *St. Joan* by Cauchon, Bishop of Beauvais, to the English Chaplain who at Joan's trial had called for her burning. Now he is old and broken by what he has done. " I did a very cruel thing once," he says, " because I did not know what cruelty was like. I had not seen it, you know. That is the great thing: you must see it." When Cauchon asks if the sufferings of our Lord were not enough for him, he says that although, as he thought, he had been greatly moved by them, it was not our Lord who redeemed him but a young woman whom he actually saw burned to death. And so the question, " Must then a Christ perish in torment in every age to save those that have no imagination? " [1]

Lack of imagination is responsible for a great deal of the sin and suffering in the world. We do and say things the result of which later appals us; we leave undone so much that we might have done and grieve that the opportunity has gone. How often we say, " Why did I do it, why did I say it? " How often we try to excuse ourselves by " if only I had known." It is as important to cultivate the imagination as it is to train the intellect and discipline the will. St. Paul knew this when he said, " All that is

---

[1] I am indebted for this illustration and for the reference below to Dick Sheppard to H. K. Luce's address on Imagination in his *The Creed of a Schoolboy*.

true, noble, just and pure—fill all your thoughts with these things." [1]

Thinking is largely based on seeing; visual aids are as old as the hills. But with television, films and picture-stories they have won a place and a power which neither parent, teacher nor publicist can ignore. To some extent they have usurped the place of the printed word and it is even conceivable that they may lead to illiteracy, which is a dismal thought. To the imagination visual aids are necessary but they may be dangerous. The devil can use them. The heavens declare the glory of God, but tempta-tion lay in the forbidden tree because it was good for food, pleasant to the eyes and desirable to make one wise. How true is the story of the Garden of Eden with its cycle of imagination awakened by visual aids, the will defeated, sin and remorse. The devil's work goes on to-day with " the sexy, the sadistic and the sordid."

But the imagination is not wholly dependent on external images. We can make our own pictures, we can see with the mind's eye. We can embark on flights of fancy into a land peopled with nameless fears and anxieties or into egotistical daydreams in which we are no longer underlings but strut along the stage as leading players to the music of applause. We are in the land of make-believe, but when we return to reality we find that we have not added one inch to our stature. There is, however, another kind of vivid imagination when we see that all the world's a stage and everyone a player on it. Dick Sheppard, known to thousands who never saw him by his broadcast addresses from St. Martin-in-the-Fields, defined imagination as " seeing the picture behind". With the mind's eye we can see the house where we were

[1] Philippians 4 : 5.

born, the face of a friend who is dead, the desk where we sat at school, the dentist's waiting-room, the beach where we bathed last summer. But we do not always see the pictures behind the lives of other people, the stories in the newspapers and all the ignorance, suffering and sin in the world. Nor do we stop to picture the results of the cruel word, the gossip and scandal passed on; we do not see the effect on others of our own lapses from the path of duty, integrity and truth.

Every day in every way we must see the picture behind. We hear of refugees and displaced persons; do we see men, women and children herded together in camps and hovels without country, home or hope? We read statistics about illegitimacy and crime; do we see behind the figures men and women, boys, girls and babies and picture the homes from which they come and the up-bringing they have had? The very words we use, those horrid, collective, abstract words like personnel, man-power, units, working classes, blind us to the fact that we are speaking of living human beings, each one unique, each one precious in the sight of God. Do we really know the people we meet? Does imagination help us to see behind the awkward or aggressive exterior, the lone-liness or timidity which cry out for friendship, sympathy and love? And how can we pray for others unless we see the picture behind, their needs and difficulties, their sorrow and pain?

Imagination is one of God's greatest gifts. Until it is developed and purged by worship we shall not easily hallow all the wonderful works of God on which he is writing his name. At its highest it is to see the world with the eyes of Christ. In the life of Jesus it was his capacity for seeing the picture behind that was the secret of the boundless sympathy which drew men to him like a magnet; for in every man he saw the image of God. The image is not always easy to see; so often it is sadly marred. But that is no excuse. There is a terrible warning for those who have no imagination. We may protest, " Lord, when was it we saw you in need and did nothing for you? " But the King will answer, " Anything you did not do for one of these, however humble, you did not do for me."

No clause in the Lord's Prayer more clearly shows that conduct follows doctrine. We have added to the Lord's Creed a doctrine of worship. Worship is essential to a man, for his life will be shaped by what he worships. Secondly, because Jesus came to give us a living image of God, we worship through Jesus Christ our Lord. This is what he meant when he said, " No one comes to the Father except by me . . . Anyone who has seen me has seen the Father." [1] Thirdly, reverence of God through Jesus must lead to reverence of ourselves and of our fellow men, for Jesus was made Man. Thereby " he has sealed human nature with a certificate of value whose validity cannot be disputed." [2] Finally, we must reverence everything on which God has written his name. This leads to a doctrine of values chief among which are the absolute values, goodness, beauty and truth. These are personal values and have their source in a personal God.

And if it seems that our thoughts have turned too much towards man, too little towards God, the answer is very simple—the Christian doctrine of man will always make

[1] John 14 : 6, 9.
[2] *The Importance of Being Human*, E. L. Mascall, p. 22.

its demands upon us whenever and wherever we hallow God's name. For the nature and destiny of man depend upon God and only through reverencing God can we find fullness of life for ourselves and see our duty to extend to others the blessings we so richly enjoy. "The fear of the Lord is the beginning of wisdom, and the knowledge of the Holy One insight." [1] Thus to hallow the name of God is not a subtle form of self-glorification, but a loving and humble self-giving and self-dedication.

[1] Proverbs 9 : 10.

V. THY KINGDOM COME

It is not the totality of the secular totalitarian State which is wrong, but the fact that it is the wrong totality. Christianity also makes totalitarian demands.

Kitson Clark, *The Kingdom of Free Men*, p. 122

I should be content to accept the old-fashioned division of religions into the two classes of world-renouncing and world-affirming. And if I were asked, " Then in which class do you put Christianity? " I should blandly reply, " Neither." Christianity stands in a class by itself. It is a world-transforming religion.

Bishop Wand, *The Mystery of the Kingdom*, p. 85

The progress of the Kingdom consists in the uprising within the hearts of men of a love and trust which answers to the Love which shines from the Cross.

William Temple, *Readings in St. John's Gospel*, Introduction, p. xxi.

" HERE BEGINS the Gospel of Jesus Christ the Son of God." So opens the Gospel of St. Mark. What was the gospel, the good news? Jesus said, " The time has come; the Kingdom of God is upon you; repent, and believe the Gospel." [1]

There has never been a systemized or carefully thought out theology of the Kingdom. Christian dogma deals with the nature of God, the person of Christ, the Church and Sacraments, and even with the nature of man; but the nature of the Kingdom forms no part of creeds or confessions. In this

[1] Mark 1 : 15.

respect they offer a sharp contrast with the Lord's own prayer, which gives a central place to the petition, " Thy Kingdom come." [1]

So says Bishop Wand, and his words underline the fact that the Lord's Prayer is the Lord's own Creed and is far more important than any creeds that men have drawn up. This clause is central: it looks back to what has gone before and forward to the clauses that follow. Back because if God is our Father and is supreme over the whole universe, if his name and all that it stands for must be reverenced, then we must work and pray for the establishment of his Kingdom on earth as it is in heaven. Forward because when he reigns in our hearts we shall want to satisfy the material needs of all men, we shall forgive as we hope to be forgiven and we shall fight against evil. As for the failure to think out all the implications of " the Kingdom of God is upon you ", that has been quite disastrous. For how can we hope to understand fully the doctrines of the Church, the sacraments, the nature of man and indeed the nature of God revealed in the person of Jesus unless we understand what he meant by the Good News of the Kingdom?

Bishop Wand defines the Kingdom of God as " the sphere of God's recognised authority ". [2] It consists of those who acknowledge and accept God's claim on them to try to fashion themselves and their lives according to his will. Thus " thy Kingdom come " is followed by " thy will be done ". There are three aspects of the Kingdom. It begins in man's heart and life, it issues in a perfected society, and it is the goal of history. Thus

---

[1] *The Mystery of the Kingdom*, p. 2.
[2] op. cit., p. 7. In what follows I have drawn freely from this book.

it begins with the individual, it must embrace all spheres of life and it is " the one far off divine event to which the whole creation moves."

It begins with the individual. The challenge comes to a man's own conscience. Jesus said, " Unless a man has been born over again he cannot see the Kingdom of God. . . . The wind blows where it wills; you hear the sound of it, but you do not know where it comes from, or where it is going. So with everyone who is born from spirit." [1] Even in these days of mass control and planning individual personality is the ultimate unit of human existence. " It remains true that the most important events in the world are probably private events, and all the important results are certainly private results." [2] And of all private events a man's conversion to God is the most important and of all private results its effects on his life will be outstanding. The man who was asked why he went to church and answered, " To show which side I'm on," may not have been " born over again "; but he was not far from the Kingdom of God. But when a man can say

> Take my life and let it be
> Consecrated, Lord, to thee,

he is a member of the Kingdom.

We need to be very careful in our thinking about the qualifications for membership in the Kingdom and about the qualities which members will show; they are often so very different from the values of the world, and sometimes indeed from what church people prize. There is plenty of evidence in the New Testament that some of the things that Jesus said and did shocked people, shocked

[1] John 3 : 3, 8.
[2] *The Kingdom of Free Men*, G. Kitson Clark, p. 193.

even the Twelve. " Not everyone who calls me ' Lord,
Lord ' will enter the Kingdom of Heaven, but only those
who do the will of my heavenly Father. When that day
comes, many will say to me, ' Lord, Lord, did we not
prophesy in your name, cast out devils in your name,
and in your name perform many miracles? ' Then I will
tell them to their face, ' I never knew you: out of my
sight, you and your wicked ways '." [1] Thus " when
Jesus had finished this discourse (the Sermon on the
Mount) the people were astounded at his teaching:
unlike their own teachers he taught with a note of
authority." [2] Of course he did, for the King of the
Kingdom was speaking, but they did not know it. What
had he been saying? He had been describing the sort
of people who would be found in the Kingdom—" those
who know that they are poor, the sorrowful, those of a
gentle spirit, who hunger and thirst to see right prevail,
who show mercy, whose hearts are pure, the peacemakers,
those who have suffered persecution for the cause of
right." [3]

Someone asked him, " Sir, are only a few to be
saved? " His answer was: " Struggle to get in
through the narrow door; for I tell you that many
will try to enter and not be able. When once the
master of the house has got up and locked the door,
you may stand outside and knock, and say, ' Sir, let
us in! ' but he will only answer, ' I do not know
where you come from.' Then you will begin to say,
' We sat at table with you and you taught in our
streets.' But he will repeat, ' I tell you, I do not

[1] Matthew 7 : 21–3.   [2] Matthew 7 : 28, 29.
[3] Matthew 5 : 3–10, The Beatitudes.

know where you come from. Out of my sight, all of you, you and your wicked ways!' There will be wailing and grinding of teeth there, when you see Abraham, Isaac and Jacob, and all the prophets, in the Kingdom of God, and yourselves thrown out. From east and west people will come, from north and south, for the feast in the Kingdom of God. Yes, and some who are now last will be first, and some who are first will be last." [1]

It was all very disturbing and it should be disturbing to-day. It is easy enough to interpret the words of Jesus as meaning that membership of the Kingdom is exclusive or inclusive, and in either case to miss his meaning. There are sects and individuals who, with preposterous arrogance and self-righteousness, count themselves alone to be " saved " to the exclusion of all others. Let them read the words quoted above and take warning. Others are so easygoing that they condone the evil in the world and in themselves and call it tolerance. They too should read their New Testament again.

Jesus did lay down one absolute condition of membership in his Kingdom. " They brought children for him to touch; and the disciples scolded them for it. But when Jesus saw this he was indignant, and said to them, ' Let the children come to me; do not try to stop them; for the Kingdom of God belongs to such as these. I tell you, whoever does not accept the Kingdom of God like a child will never enter it.' " [2] Like a child. How does a child accept anyone or anything? With absolute trust, sincerity and simplicity. We cannot enter the Kingdom unless we trust Jesus absolutely. He is the Lord of all

[1] Luke 13 : 23–30.   [2] Mark 10 : 13–15.

life and of our life; he speaks with a note of authority and we must accept him at his word. We cannot enter the kingdom unless we are absolutely sincere. There can be no reservations, no double talk, like the prayer which Augustine is supposed to have said as a young man, " O Lord, make me pure, but not yet." We cannot enter without simplicity. Doubts there may be, for many people are agnostic to some extent; and simplicity does not mean that we should ever violate our intellectual integrity. Simplicity is not simpleness; to put off the old man does not mean to put on the old woman. Nor is it credulity which abandons reason. But reason and intellect are not all. Gore defined faith as " instinct illuminated by reason." Simplicity is that instinctive trust which is seen in its purest form in childhood, when " heaven lies about us in our infancy". It is seen in Job when he said, " Though he slay me yet will I trust in him." [1] It is seen in the father who was pleading for Jesus to heal his son, " I have faith; help me where faith falls short." [2] It is seen in the penitent criminal who said, " Jesus, remember me when you come to your throne." [3]

One thing is quite certain. There must be decision and we have to make it. The pursuit of the Hound of Heaven is relentless; he will never give up. Some day, somehow we must stop running away and face him. There is perhaps no finer or more intimate description of the final struggle than this:

You must picture me alone in that room at Magdalen, night after night, feeling, whenever my mind lifted even for a second from my work, the steady, unrelenting approach of Him whom I so earnestly desired

[1] Job 13 : 15. A.V.   [2] Mark 9 : 24.
[3] Luke 23 : 42.

not to meet. That which I greatly feared had at last come upon me. In the Trinity Term of 1929 I gave in, and admitted that God was God, and knelt and prayed: perhaps, that night, the most dejected and reluctant convert in England. I did not then see what is now the most shining and obvious thing; the Divine humility which will accept a convert even on such terms. The Prodigal Son at least walked home on his own feet. But who can duly adore that Love which will open the high gates to a prodigal who is brought in kicking, struggling, re-sentful, and darting his eyes in every direction for a chance of escape? The words *compelle intrare*, compel them to come in, have been so abused by wicked men that we shudder at them; but, properly understood, they plumb the depth of Divine mercy. The hard-ness of God is kinder than the softness of men, and his compulsion is our liberation. [1]

The Kingdom is made up of its members. It is a society of individuals, but not of individualists. Someone once said that there are three conversions in a man's life, first to Christ, then to the Church and then back to the world. A man cannot rest in the first stage, concerned only with his own salvation. He must pass on to see that the Church is God's instrument for bringing in his kingdom. Nor can he stay in the second stage, for that would be to confine the Kingdom to the Church. The third stage —back to the world—is our second aspect of the King-dom which is that it is to be expressed in a perfected order of society. We shall have to discuss both this and the relation of the Church to the Kingdom more fully later

[1] C. S. Lewis, *Surprised by Joy*, pp. 182, 3.

on. Here we must note that the Kingdom of God is in sharp contrast with the Kingdom of the World which is society apart from God. It is the godless society, whereas the Kingdom is society organised under the direction of God. Of course that order is not fully in being, far from it; nor do we know if it will ever be achieved in time. What we have to do is to act as if it can be, remembering that we are taught to pray " thy will be done in *earth*." Every sphere of man's activity and interest must be brought within the Kingdom. " All social relationships are to be brought under his sway; marriage, the family, the nation, the government, industrial and political life. The Lord of all life must be obeyed in all life." [1]

The third aspect is that the Kingdom will be found to perfection in the " world-without-end". Thus it is the goal of history. If history has a meaning and a purpose, and is not just a record of facts, then it is the Kingdom which tells us what that meaning is. It points to a perfection stored up in heaven. Everything we do here and now is judged in that light. The importance of this aspect is that it gives purpose and meaning to life. " The sphere of history is the sphere of human responsibility" [2] and we can be assured that all our strivings and struggles have dignity and value because they serve a purpose which is eternal, world-without-end.

All this is but the barest sketch of the teaching of Jesus on the Kingdom of God. It is illustrated by his Sermon on the Mount, by numerous parables and most of all by his own life; for he came to inaugurate the Kingdom and where he was there was the Kingdom. It is his own life, his attitude to the world of people and his scale of

[1] Wand, op. cit., p. 48.   [2] Wand, op. cit., p. 14.

values, which show us more clearly than anything else
what the Kingdom means. He offered what men have
always longed for, and still long for—the reign of happiness, peace and community, whether they have called it
the Messianic hope, Utopia or the Golden Age. It is at
least possible that if Christians had gained a clearer conception of the Kingdom of God and had preached and
practised it—and they were told to go into all the world
—we might have been spared some of the disastrous substitutes that men have provided for themselves. The
corruption of the best is always the worst kind of corruption. The substitutes end in tragedy: either they can
succeed in establishing a " kingdom " by means which
destroy the ends to which they aim; or they fail and leave
behind thousands of disillusioned, resentful people,
cheated of their hopes.

The obvious examples are Fascism, Nazism and
Communism, or any other form of statism. These hold
out high hopes of great material blessings and actually
achieve much. There is plenty of proof of this. There
is, for instance, something Messianic in the teaching of
Karl Marx, and he did have a burning passion for social
justice. But the means employed to achieve the ends
have been, and are, utterly disastrous to man. The
individual is nothing, the State everything, and God is
eliminated. People become mere pawns ; they can be
liquidated at will by the process of social surgery. Hitler
was prepared to do away with all Jews and did in
fact kill six million of them. The record of these
substitutes is too well known to need repetition.

It is often asked whether we in the West, with all our
failures to live up to our Christian heritage, have any
right to criticise others? It is a fair question and there

will be something to say later on about these failures. But here we must note that there is a heritage of the West and it is a Christian heritage. Dr. Visser t'Hooft, Secretary of the World Council of Churches, has pointed out that there are at least four precious things which we still possess from this heritage. There is the possibility of discussion. This is important, not only because truth often springs from conflict of opinion, but because monologue gives birth to solipsism—it encloses the movement, the party, the church in immense solitude. Free speech is essential, not because men are so wise that by discussion they necessarily find the truth, but because men are so wicked and stupid that unless contradicted they will take their own voices for the voice of a god. Secondly, we believe in the independence of truth. One chosen ideology to which education and every thing else is aligned is utterly foreign to us, but it is the way of every form of statism. " The Christian must welcome truth from whatever quarter it comes, for his Lord is the Truth as well as the Way and the Life. A sound Christian theology insists that the love of truth is as important as the practice of truthfulness." [1] We are in danger of forgetting this when we talk of " protestant " or " catholic " or " scientific " truth and we must beware. But we are still far removed—thank God—from the Communist doctrine of expediency in which the truth of to-day may become the lie of to-morrow. Thirdly, we still retain the possibility of responsible life, and without this there is no freedom. Statism robs man of a truly responsible life and so enslaves him. Lastly, we are able to keep a sense of proportion between what really counts

[1] Archbishop Ramsey, quoted in *God and the Rich Society*, Munby, p. 157.

and what is secondary. This is the difference between the absolute and the relative. Europe has refused to consider man merely as a political animal. Thus the opponents of Hitler were opposing heresy and they knew it. Statism leads to the denial that there are absolute values and absolute moral imperatives. It leads to the idolatry of the system or the leader. Some of the young people in Russia know that they are lost.

> " You are Christians," some of them said to me, " you have had your chance; you know what is good and what is bad; you know how to act in life. . . . But we do not know. One day a thing is white, the next it is black." . . . This nostalgia for transcendent principles according to which they can direct their personal lives leads some of them to turn towards Christianity, and even to convert. The starting point of almost every religious quest is a stirring of conscience in the face of injustice or deceit. [1]

It has been worth while to pause and look at the blessings we so richly enjoy, for some people are ready to decry our Western heritage whilst enjoying its fruits. A short sojourn behind the Curtain might bring them to their senses. Others talk as if the West were already the Kingdom of God on earth; they are blind to our failures. The best cure for both these attitudes is to try to extend to others the blessings of our heritage; in doing so we may give more thought to the values in which they rest and to the dangers in our own manner of life which threaten them. But one thing is quite essen-

[1] "*Quel témoignage peut toucher les esprits soviétiques?*" Hélène Peltier-Zamoyska. Quoted in *God and the Soviets*, Constantin de Grünwald, p. 225.

tial; our giving must not be from cupboard-love. There are plenty of people who talk about " a battle for people's minds ", meaning that the best insurance against Communism is to win over the peoples of Asia and Africa by helping them. But

> the struggle that interests them is that against disease, want and ignorance. It ought to be the most obvious of all human truths that if I give a man a steel works or a dam because I want him to think like me or " to be on my side," he will take the things and spit in my eye. This is the morality of the sugar-daddy. But if I give him the very same things because I want him to be richer and healthier, without thought of my own advantage, he will take them and be thankful. He will not forget my action and, *provided I had no thought of such a thing in my mind*, I will in due course receive my reward and my advantage." [1]

This is only another way of saying that the blessings of the Kingdom of God on earth—and these blessings include all the humanitarian influences and actions which it inspires—must be extended from no ulterior motives, but simply because they are meant for all men under the sun. We are commanded to carry the Good News of Christianity to all the world because it is the truth and for no other reason.

In all the substitutes for the Kingdom of God there is one fundamental error. They are man-made kingdoms in which God has no place; and when God has been dispossessed and man enthroned in his place, strange as it seems, the sanctity of man as man is lost. Man builds

[1] *Strategy for Survival*, Wayland Young, p. 50.

his own kingdom and commits suicide in doing so. Schemes for establishing the Golden Age which eliminate God sound the death-knell of man himself. There is also another reason why they are bound to fail. They ignore sin, they refuse to recognise that there is anything wrong with human nature and that man needs redemption. Man can raise himself by his own shoe-strings. Nothing is impossible. This mistake is shared by humanists with whom Christians have so much in common. They believe in the inevitability of progress of man by his own efforts and in his own power. More education, science, technology, hygiene and so on, and he is in control of his own evolution. There is no doubt about the immense powers within our reach; but there still remains the question—how shall we use them? It is not enough to know *what* men can do; nor is it necessarily wise that he should do everything that is within his power. He has got to ask not only *what* but *why*. In other words, the first question is what purpose is he seeking, what is the end he is aiming at. Charles Morgan illustrates this by the following story or parable. He was visited by a young American nuclear physicist who had just been witnessing some interesting experiments in Europe on a frog's egg. A frog's egg had five areas or fields of energy and it had been possible to neutralise one of these fields. The egg was hatched. The tadpole seemed normal, but the resulting frog had only three legs. This opened up boundless possibilities, for if you could put something out, why not put something in? It was a long hope of turning bad citizens into good. Charles Morgan was not enthusiastic and was asked why not. " Because," he said, " I don't want to put it into anyone's power to turn a child into a hyena." After a good deal of thought his friend said, " It all depends, doesn't it, not so much on what one thinks that men can do as on what one believes that a man is? " [1] The ultimate blasphemy is mind possession and control. Men cannot be used as means to an end, for each human life is an end in itself. We speak and read a great deal about freedom and the rights of the individual, but it is worth remembering that " no guarantee of freedom of belief, or of any other form of freedom, is worth anything when it is given by men who accept no philosophy of freedom and do not respect any of the values which such a philosophy teaches." [2] We shall always be in danger of using others as means to an end until we ourselves have faced the questions—What am I for, why am I here? Freedom from what, to do what, to be what? Until a man does this, either he will live without any purpose at all or he will make himself his own god and follow, not his own will, but his wilfulness, for unredeemed man is not in control of himself. Constantly he has to admit, " I discover this principle: that when I want to do right, only the wrong is within my reach," and he finds himself " fighting against the law that my reason approves." [3] The result in either case will spell chaos for himself and danger to others.

" Master, I was afraid, and I went and hid your gold in the ground." [4] This perhaps is the trouble with many of us. " Fear of freedom, fear of truth and fear of living are closely linked in respect of a faith which claims to be the Way, the Truth and the Life." [5] And yet Jesus

[1] *Liberties of the Mind*, pp. 12–16.

[2] Kitson Clark, *The Kingdom of Free Men*, p. 42.

[3] Romans 7 : 21, 23.   [4] Matthew 25 : 25.

[5] *The Spoil of the Violent*, Emmanuel Mounier, p. 84. This short book of 85 pages is a vigorous and refreshing plea for adventurous living.

said, " Ever since the coming of John the Baptist the Kingdom of Heaven has been subjected to violence and violent men are seizing it." [1]   When he came and announced the Good News of the Kingdom, people received him with enthusiasm; they jostled one another to get into the Kingdom. John the Baptist was the last prophet under the old régime of the Law. Jesus did not abrogate the Law, but he offered the Kingdom of Free Men: " Go and tell John what you have seen and heard: how the blind recover their sight, the lame walk, the lepers are clean, the deaf hear, the dead are raised to life, the poor are hearing the good news." [2] All this is in glaring contrast with the life which is purposeless, self-centred, wilful and uncontrolled. The life devoted to the work of the King and his Kingdom is an adventure in which there is no room for fear of freedom, truth and living. It is creative co-operation with the will of God, and where and how that will lead us must be the subject of the next chapter.

It is superfluous to say that we have not given a full account of the doctrine of the Kingdom which is beyond the scope of this book and the ability of its author. Moreover " thy Kingdom come " is incomplete without the next clause. But we have at least made some additions to the Lord's Creed.

The Kingdom must start with the individual; there is a doctrine of Conversion. No one can enter the Kingdom until he has turned to Jesus and committed his life to him in simple but absolute trust. This step is not easy,

[1] Matthew 11 : 12. The parallel passage is Luke 16 : 16.
[2] Luke 7 : 22.

> For, though I knew his love Who followed,
>   Yet was I sore adread
> Lest, having Him, I must have naught beside.[1]

But thousands have taken this step and have found that they have entered the Kingdom of Free Men.

Secondly, the Kingdom must embrace all life; it is a totalitarian doctrine, and the only one of its kind that a man can accept. Its total demands are permissible because it alone can prove the truth in the paradox " whose service is perfect freedom." There is no religious department of life, nothing can be outside the sphere of the Kingdom's influence. Thus it is concerned not only with the conversion of individuals, but of groups and classes. It must transform civilisations and cultures, politics and economics and all the conditions of life under which men live. In this sense it is a doctrine of Society. This does not mean that there are specifically Christian programmes to effect the transformation, but that Christians who are members of the Kingdom must play their part as " salt to the world ".[2] The Kingdom of God " is like yeast which a woman took and mixed with half a hundredweight of flour till it was all leavened." [3] Christians have no business to try to force Christian ideals on to a world which is not ready to accept them; but they have a duty to try to create a climate of opinion and conditions which will prepare the way for the Kingdom.

Thirdly, if the Kingdom means transformation, there is inherent in it a doctrine of continuity which neither renounces this world nor is confined to it. We cannot

---

[1] " The Hound of Heaven," Francis Thompson.
[2] Matthew 5 : 13.   [3] Luke 13 : 21.

renounce the world to which Jesus said " the Kingdom of God is upon you"—a world for which he lived and died and which in his risen life he has never deserted. Nor must our vision be restricted solely to this world, for Jesus never promised the perfected Kingdom here on earth; but he did say that its final victory was assured. Members of the Kingdom are citizens of two worlds and there is no gulf between them. The very qualities he demands for membership and the blessings he promises bear on them the stamp of eternal validity and truth. Thus this doctrine of continuity is the doctrine of Eternal Life, and the Kingdom is present, future and without end because the King is the same yesterday, to-day and for ever. We have to work here and now that God's holy name may be glorified and his blessed Kingdom enlarged, in sure and certain hope that life here is not the end. Even if this present body and this present world of ours must pass away, we shall live on and all our efforts will not be lost, but will be woven into the tapestry of the Kingdom of Heaven which is beyond time and place, when " the universe itself is to be freed from the shackles of mortality and enter upon the liberty and splendour of the children of God." [1]

" Therefore, my beloved brothers, stand firm and immovable, and work for the Lord always, work without limit, since you know that in the Lord your labour cannot be lost." [2]

---

[1] Romans 8 : 21.   [2] I Corinthians 15 : 58.

VI. THY WILL BE DONE IN EARTH
AS IT IS IN HEAVEN

Whoever wishes to take up the problem of a Christian ethic must first be confronted at once with a demand which is quite without parallel. He must from the outset discard as irrelevant the two questions which alone impel him to concern himself with the problem of ethics, " How can I be good? " and " How can I do good? ", and instead of these he must ask the utterly and totally different question, " What is the will of God? "

Bonhoeffer, Ethics, p. 55

It is a mutilated obedience which consists in being very religious and at the same time socially irresponsible; it is also a mutilated obedience which combines zest for improving the lot of mankind with indifference to the Lord God in whom we all live and move and have our being.

Vidler, Christian Belief and This World, p. 91

There is no part of the world, be it never so forlorn and never so godless, which is not accepted by God and reconciled with God in Jesus Christ.

Bonhoeffer, Ethics, p. 71

HOW do we discover the will of God? There are four well recognised ways—the Bible, the life and teaching of Jesus, the guidance of the Holy Spirit and the authority of the Church. It would be absurd, however, to suggest that God can only make his will known along certain recognised lines of communication. *We* cannot dispense with them, but we must be ready for him to speak to us in all sorts of ways. If " the religious moment flowers from the practical,"[1] so does the will of God; and "there is a sense in which he is at the tip of my pen, my spade, my brush, my needle—of my heart and of my thought." [2]

There are three books which have probably had more influence than any others—*Das Kapital, Mein Kampf* and the Bible. We are still living under the influence of the first and last; and although the reign of *Mein Kampf* has ended, its influence perhaps is still to be feared. The Bible can be a dangerous book; it can so easily be misused and misunderstood. The use of "proof texts", the belief in "verbal inspiration", the failure to recognise that some parts of the Bible must carry less weight than others, that contradictions and even unchristian ideas are to be expected and above all that the New Testament must carry infinitely more authority than the Old, all these may prove to be stumbling blocks to a proper understanding of the Bible and therefore of the will of God.

The Bible is on God's side the progressive revelation of himself, his nature, his character and his will. On the manward side it can be a progressive discovery of God and his will. "When in former times God spoke to our forefathers, he spoke in fragmentary and varied fashion through the prophets. But in this the final age he has spoken to us in the Son." [3] In these words is stated quite clearly the progressive and preparatory revelation in the Old Testament and the authority of the New. We cannot fully appreciate the New without the Old, and we can certainly never learn the doctrines which must rule our lives simply from the Old. Thus, to take one or two illustrations, in the Old Testament we find the great

[1] *Only One Way Left*, George MacLeod, p. 160.
[2] *Le Milieu Divin*, Teilhard de Chardin, p. 37.
[3] Hebrews 1 : 1.

fundamental moral laws which form the basis of any society. We need not be surprised or disconcerted to learn that these are to be found in some form elsewhere and even earlier than biblical times. This only goes to show that they are universal and therefore surely God's plan and will for all societies. These laws Jesus never abrogated, but he did amplify their scope and enrich their meaning. Again, it is possible to assume from the Old Testament that certain people are destined by God to an inferior position, and presumably Apartheid rests on this doctrine. There was a time, no doubt, when exclusiveness was necessary to avoid contamination by heathen customs and idolatry. But progressive understanding of the will of God and of the teaching of Jesus should break all barriers of class and race and colour. Even in the New Testament there may be misunderstanding of the " progressiveness " of Jesus himself. For example, the fact that Jesus chose only men as his immediate " ministry " does not necessarily mean that women must for ever be barred from the ordained ministry of the Church. St. Paul's attitude to women is an even less valid argument. " I wish you to understand," he says, " that, while every man has Christ for his Head, woman's head is man. . . . A man has no need to cover his head, because man is the image of God, and the mirror of his glory, whereas woman reflects the glory of man." [1] " As in all congregations of God's people, women should not address the meeting. They have no licence to speak, but should keep their place as the law directs. If there is something they want to know, they can ask their husbands at home. It is a shocking thing that a woman should address the congregation." [2] When

[1] I Corinthians 11 : 3, 7.   [2] I Corinthians 14 : 34, 35.

Jesus lived in the world it would have been quite impossible to choose women to occupy the position of the
Twelve; and yet he does seem to have gone beyond the
conventions of the times in allowing a small devoted
band of women to minister to his needs. St. Paul's
attitude reflects the times in which he lived and the
customs of the people for whom he was legislating. There
may be valid, practical reasons why women should not
be ordained to the ministry, but the fact that Jesus did
not commission women to carry on his work and that
St. Paul summarily dismissed any such suggestion is
not conclusive. Unhappily the Church has remained
stubbornly anti-feminist in not seeing the need for, and
the scope of, a ministry of women. For them the opportunities the Church offers are pathetically meagre and in
glaring contrast with the many openings in the secular
world. In this the Church is out of line with one of the
most important developments of the last hundred years
—the emancipation of women.

But the difficulties and possible misunderstandings
which can arise in studying the Bible are as nothing
compared with its riches. Herein we can find the will
of God. By it alone men have been converted to God.
Through it God speaks to each one of us, just as truly as
when the prophets say, " The word of the Lord came to
me saying . . ." And there is not the slightest doubt
that if it can be said that many people to-day are not so
much immoral as ignorant of morality, that ignorance
can largely be traced to neglect of the Bible. For how
can we know the will of God unless we are steeped in the
Bible, and, most of all, in the New Testament which
gives us the life and teaching of the Lord of all life?

There is a story told of a man who in World War I was

just going on leave from the trenches, when a chance shot mortally wounded him. His last words were, " Isn't that just like God? " God, the Almighty Fate, holding out blessings with one hand and snatching them away with the other? But the writer adds that no man would ever have said, " Isn't that just like Jesus Christ?"[1] That precisely illustrates the importance of the life and teaching of Jesus Christ; for Jesus came to reveal the nature of God and his will for man. Nothing which would be incompatible with the character of Jesus can find a place in the character of God. All that Jesus showed us by his life and by his words must be the will of God. This is not to suggest that we have clear cut directions for every occasion and clear cut answers to every problem. But we have great guiding principles and minds to apply them—and we have a Life which is the Light of the World. There is a simple little parable which reminds us that we are human beings capable of reason and action, not puppets. Two men were walking in a forest when they met a lion. One said, " Brother, let us kneel and pray to God that he will deliver us." " Not so," said the other, " when he has given us legs to run away with."

Nothing can take the place of a constant study of the New Testament. If we are steeped in it, we shall not on each and every occasion have to seek the will of God. We shall begin to order our lives in such a way that the natural reaction to any given circumstances will be in tune with God's will. The old superstition of opening the Bible at random and sticking a pin on a page to find the answer to a puzzle was as unchristian as it was ludicrous. But it is just as unchristian, and indeed arrogant, to suppose that we can have the mind of Christ if we

[1] *Be of Good Cheer*, W. P. G. McCormick, p. 10.

neglect to study his life and teaching. And in this we are helped enormously to-day by modern translations, of which *The New English Bible* is the latest. Many people prefer the old versions. They are familiar with its language and the beauty of it. But this familiarity is perhaps the chief reason why we need a modern translation. The old language, with its archaisms, can obscure the meaning and familiarity and can easily blunt the challenge of the meaning. Here are a few illustrations taken at random. In each pair the first is from the Authorised Version, the second from *The New English Bible*. Which presents the clearer meaning and challenge?

The light shineth in darkness; and the darkness comprehended it not.
The light shines on in the dark, and the darkness has never quenched it.[1]

Take heed that ye do not your alms before men.
Be careful not to make a show of your religion before men.[2]

Had compassion.
His heart went out to him.[3]

Ye cannot serve God and mammon.
You cannot serve God and Money.[4]

If any man will come after me, let him deny himself, and take up his cross daily, and follow me.
If anyone wishes to be a follower of mine, he must leave self behind; day after day he must take up his cross, and come with me.[5]

[1] John 1 : 5.   [2] Matthew 6 : 1.
[3] Luke 15 : 20.   [4] Luke 16 : 13.
[5] Luke 9 : 23.

Why beholdest thou the mote that is in thy brother's eye, but perceivest not the beam that is in thine own eye?

Why do you look at the speck of sawdust in your brother's eye, with never a thought for the great plank in your own? [1]

The bowels of the saints are refreshed by thee, brother.

Through you, my brother, God's people have been much refreshed. [2]

Charity suffereth long, and is kind; charity envieth not; charity vaunteth not itself, is not puffed up. Doth not behave itself unseemly, seeketh not her own, is not easily provoked, thinketh no evil; rejoiceth not in iniquity, but rejoiceth in the truth: beareth all things, believeth all things, hopeth all things, endureth all things.

Love is patient; love is kind and envies no one. Love is never boastful, nor conceited, nor rude; never selfish, not quick to take offence. Love keeps no score of wrongs; does not gloat over other men's sins, but delights in the truth. There is nothing that love cannot face; there is no limit to its faith, its hope, and its endurance. [3]

Be not conformed to this world: but be ye transformed by the renewing of your mind, that ye may prove what is that good, and acceptable, and perfect, will of God.

Adapt yourselves no longer to the pattern of this present world, but let your minds be remade, and

[1] Luke 6 : 41.   [2] Philemon 7.
[3] I Corinthians 13 : 4–7.

your whole nature thus transformed. Then you will
be able to discern the will of God, and to know what
is good, acceptable and perfect.[1]

No one will wish to deny that the language of the
Authorised Version has helped to shape our daily speech
and our oratory. But if we are " to discern the will of
God, and to know what is good, acceptable, and perfect," we should be prepared to use a modern translation. And it is more than likely that opposition comes
—consciously or unconsciously—from a reluctance to face
the challenge that is bound to come when we read the
New Testament in everyday language. " Mammon " is
comfortably obscure, " money " is not. " Not to do
one's alms before men " may mean that a collection bag
is preferable to a plate or to Christian Stewardship.
" Not to make a show of religion " has a far wider
meaning. To examine ourselves by I Corinthians 13 in
modern dress can be a very searching experience. " Not
to be conformed to this world " can seem to be sufficiently
vague to leave little impression on us. " Not to adapt
ourselves to the pattern of this present world " means
exactly what it says—do not lower your standards to
meet the standards of a world which has not yet become
the kingdom of God.

But even when we are honestly trying to discover the
will of God through the Bible and the life and teaching
of Jesus, there are two difficulties. The first is, broadly
speaking, the problem of suffering. How can we face and
explain the great natural disasters—earthquakes, hurri-
canes, plague, famine and so on—and the pain and
suffering of the innocent? Are they the will of God?

[1] Romans 12 : 2.

Here we must confine ourselves to a few comments on a subject on which many a book has been written.[1] The first thing to repeat is that nothing which is incompatible with the loving character of Jesus can be compatible with the will of God. Jesus *did* go about healing the sick. He *did* say that the woman with a spinal curvature was bound by Satan. He *did* deny that a man's blindness from birth was due to his or his parents' sin. Thus it is wrong—and indeed blasphemous—when we are faced with some appalling tragedy to say that it is God's will. Here we can trust our own instinct. Nothing can be good before God which is evil in our eyes. But the corollary of this is that God can and does bring good out of evil; he can transform tragedy into triumph. This is the meaning of the Cross; and the triumph will depend upon the way tragedy affects us. If it " gets us down ", it will remain tragedy for us. If it can make us stronger and braver in character and teach us more sympathy and compassion, that is triumph. It is important to differentiate between acceptance of, and resignation to, suffering. We must never cease to fight it. This surely is included in " thy will be done *in earth* ". Resignation leads to apathy and inaction and indifference to the sufferings of others. The contrast is well brought out in the modern version of a well-known hymn. The first three verses of the latter are sufficient to show that it gives a picture of folded hands and pious resignation.

> My God, my Father, while I stray,
> Far from my home, on life's rough way,
> O teach me from my heart to say,
>   " Thy Will be done."

[1] See Austin Farrer's excellent *Love Almighty and Ills Unlimited*.

Though dark my path, and sad my lot,
Let me be still and murmur not,
Or breathe the prayer divinely taught,
    " Thy Will be done."

What though in lonely grief I sigh
For friends beloved no longer nigh,
Submissive would I still reply,
    " Thy Will be done." [1]

The new version breathes challenge, faith and hope in
every line. It is a battle cry of the Church Militant here
on earth.

My God, my Father, make me strong
When tasks of life seem hard and long,
To greet them with this triumph song:
    Thy will be done.

Draw from my timid eyes the veil,
To show, where earthly forces fail,
Thy power and love must still prevail,
    Thy will be done.

With confident and humble mind,
Freedom in service I would find,
Praying through every toil assigned,
    Thy will be done.

Things deemed impossible I dare,
Thine is the call and thine the care,
Thy wisdom shall the way prepare,
    Thy will be done.

[1] Charlotte Elliott in *Hymns Ancient and Modern*, No. 264.

All power is here and round me now,
Faithful I stand in rule and vow,
While 'tis not I, but ever thou;
    Thy will be done.

Heaven's music chimes the glad days in,
Hope soars beyond death, pain, and sin,
Faith shouts in triumph, Love must win,
    Thy will be done.[1]

The other difficulty is when sincere and honest Christians differ as to what ought to be done, often to the extent of holding diametrically opposed views. If Christians are trying to follow the will of God, how can they disagree? If they differ, how can they both be right? And yet the plain fact is that they do differ: one has only to think of pacifism, unilateral nuclear disarmament, contraception, Christians in different political parties, and the controversy over such things as gambling, blood sports, drink, Sunday observance, and so on. There is no doubt that this is a real difficulty, and sometimes a scandal, to many.

The first thing to note is that probably Christians do not disagree about the will of God, but about the way in which his will is to be fulfilled. The disagreement is about means, not ends. Thus pacifists and non-pacifists alike know that God's will is peace, and those who abhor the use of contraceptives see the urgency of the population problem just as clearly as those who teach "family planning" by artificial means. In the same way it is not to be supposed that those Christians who enjoy gambling and drink are not alive to the dangers of excess. They will probably argue that these are innocent

[1] Frederick Mann in *Songs of Praise*, No. 583.

enjoyments, but like many other pleasures over-indulgence can be very harmful and therefore sinful. Christians in politics are bound to follow the political theory which they believe will lead to economic and social improvement. But there is no political theory in the Gospels. Thus we need not be surprised that Christians disagree about means, so long as we are careful to respect one another and agree that we are trying to fulfil the will of God. The real harm comes when we vilify the motives of those with whom we disagree.

But when all this has been said, we are bound to admit with sadness and shame that if we were better Christians there would be far less disagreement. In other words, we are all very imperfect listeners to the voice of God and learners of his will. If we are not in regular, daily communion with God, if indeed our praying consists of too much talking to him and too little listening for him to speak to us, then his message may become distorted. The marvel is that God can and does use even these distortions. For example, if we think that in the present situation pacifism is a distortion of the duty of a Christian, we have at least got to admit that the witness of pacifists is a valuable contribution in awakening our consciences to the evils of war and its causes. Similarly a teetotaller calls us to remember that drunkenness is beastly and dangerous. It is a good thing that there are always people who hold extreme views, however much we may disagree with them.

Why are we not better Christians? Because example is not enough. Indeed, to try to follow the example of Jesus without the power to do so could very easily lead to despair. But the power is available all the time. Jesus said, " I will ask the Father, and he will give you another to be your Advocate, who will be with you for ever—the Spirit of truth." The words following show clearly what he meant: " I will not leave you bereft; I am coming back to you." [1] All that Jesus had revealed of the Father, all that he had brought in himself, all this is the continuing work of the Holy Spirit. At first the disciples did not fully understand what he meant, but at Pentecost full realisation dawned upon them. He never had left them, he was with them all the time. This transformed weak men who had deserted him into men of power who, caring not a jot of their own safety, spoke out boldly in public in the same city where Jesus had been arrested and killed. To Paul and his companions directions came from the Holy Spirit or the Spirit of Jesus—it was the same One. " They were prevented by the Holy Spirit from delivering the message in the province of Asia; . . . they tried to enter Bithynia; but the Spirit of Jesus would not allow them." [2] This Holy Spirit is both guide and power; he transforms " I would " into " I can ". " Because I live, you too will live; then you will know that I am in my Father, and you in me and I in you." [3] This is the mystery of which St. Paul so often speaks. " The secret is this: Christ in you, the hope of a glory to come." [4] " I have strength for anything through him who gives me power." [5] " The life that I now live is not my life, but the life which Christ lives in me." [6] It is indeed a mystery, but all truth ends in mystery. It means that we can receive the indwelling Spirit of God to show us his will and to give us the power to do it.

[1] John 14 : 16, 18. [2] Acts 16 : 6, 7.
[3] John 14 : 19. [4] Colossians 1 : 27.
[5] Philippians 4 : 13. [6] Galatians 2 : 20.

My spirit longs for thee
Within my troubled breast,
Though I unworthy be
Of so divine a Guest.

Of so divine a Guest
Unworthy though I be,
Yet has my heart no rest
Until it come from thee.

Unless it come from thee,
In vain I look around;
In all that I can see
No rest is to be found.[1]

A guest does not come uninvited, and we should be incapable of inviting " so divine a Guest " unless we had some faculty which corresponds with him. It is of the essence of human nature that it has this correspondence with God, and in the seeking and doing of his will we call it conscience. " Man's conscience is the lamp of the Eternal flashing into his inmost soul." [2] There is a moral instinct within man corresponding to the divine initiative.

Liberty of conscience is one of the great liberties to be guarded and respected. Ultimately we are responsible to God and to God alone. What the Lord tells us to do, we must do. " The lion has roared; who will not fear? The Lord God has spoken; who can but prophesy? " [3] " O Nebuchadnezzar, we have no need to answer you in

---

[1] J. Byron, *English Hymnal*, No. 443.
[2] Moffatt's translation of Proverbs 20 : 27, quoted by Gore, *The Philosophy of the Good Life*, p. 255.
[3] Amos 3 : 8.

this matter. If it be so, our God whom we serve is able to deliver us from the burning fiery furnace and he will deliver us out of your hand, O King. But if not, be it known to you, O King, that we will not serve your gods or worship the golden image which you have set up." [1] These are grand words and they are echoed in the Acts of the Apostles. " Is it right in God's eyes for us to obey you rather than God? Judge for yourselves. We cannot possibly give up speaking of things we have seen and heard." [2]

But there is the danger which we all have to guard against of mistaking our own personal views and preferences for the will of God. Many a person decides on a course of action, tells God about it and calls on him for support instead of trying to find out what God wants him to do. This is a piece of unconscious arrogance, none the less dangerous because the person " means well." There is also the arrogance of the man who claims that his own personal guidance is infallibly the will of God. Those who have to deal with prospective ordinands do from time to time meet the young man who, in the opinion of a Selection Board, after the most careful consideration, is not recommended for training and yet who utterly refuses to accept the decision. The followers of Moral Rearmament are pledged to a daily " quiet time " in which to seek guidance. But this " guidance " does at times lead them into similar claims to infallibility and to the preposterous idea that salvation is only through M.R.A. There must be some authority to which appeal can be made. Conscience is not ready made, for conscience means moral consciousness and like every other aptitude the appreciation of right and wrong must be

[1] Daniel 3 : 16-18.   [2] Acts 4 : 19, 20.

cultivated. And this—the most delicate and sensitive of all gifts—has to be nursed and educated in an environment and atmosphere in which it can develop and grow to maturity. This is what the Church is for; membership in the Church provides both the authority to which private judgment can be referred and the environment in which conscience can be stimulated and grow.

The Church is the Body of Christ. It is an organism, not an organisation. It is a living thing drawing its life from Christ its Head. It is a fellowship of Christian people, the repository of Christian experience, the guardian of the Christian Faith. If the Church is all this, then it must carry authority to interpret the will of God. Actually the Church of England never has been sufficiently a teaching Church and therefore it seems to have little authority over its members. In consequence it rarely makes authoritative statements, but leaves a very great deal to individual judgment. Its comprehensiveness makes this inevitable. But if a person is a live member of the Church of England, worshipping regularly, receiving the sacraments, following the Christian Year in the Prayer Book, the Bible readings of the lectionary, the sermons of the clergy, he cannot fail to grow in the knowledge of God and his will. Moreover if he will avail himself of the numerous additional ways in which he can sharpen his intellect and his conscience —through reading, study groups, discussions, teaching missions and the like—he will inevitably be led to play his part as a member of the responsible society which the Church should be. He will be ready to check his personal guidance by submitting it to the test of the teaching of the Church and the authority of those commissioned to give it. Where there is no clear authority to direct him, he will at least be ready to seek advice and listen to others who hold views which conflict with his own.

These then are ways in which we may seek to know the will of God—the Bible, the life and teaching of Jesus, the Holy Spirit of Truth and the Church. No longer can we say, " Verily thou art a God that hidest thyself." When John spoke of the coming of Jesus, he said, " The real light which enlightens every man was even then coming into the world," [1] and nothing has ever quenched it. So we pray, " Lead kindly Light, lead thou me on."

We have still to consider the words " in earth as it is in heaven ". Once again we come face to face with the Incarnation. God in Jesus came into this world which is God's world. He came to redeem men in their total relationships, and therefore he must be concerned with conditions here and now. We have to try to make this world the Kingdom of God. Life here is a school for character and what we do and become is important because we are being shaped for eternity. But this does not mean that conditions of life here are only a means to an end. They have an importance in their own right because somehow all that is achieved here and all that is called material will, if it is built into the fabric of the Kingdom of God on earth, be built into the Kingdom of God in heaven. The difference between " in earth " and " in heaven " is not one of time and place, nor can we draw a sharp dividing line between the material and the spiritual, because life is all one and Life Eternal starts here. We are already " citizens of heaven," [2] but we cannot contract out of our citizenship of this world. Jesus said, " You are salt to the world . . . you are light for all the world." [3]   " If any man sets aside even the

[1] John 1 : 9.   [2] Philippians 3 : 20.   [3] Matthew 5 : 13, 14.

least of the Law's demands and teaches others to do the
same, he will have the lowest place in the Kingdom of
Heaven." [1] St. Paul, who reminded his readers of their
heavenly citizenship, who said that Jesus would " trans-
figure the body belonging to your humble state "[2] and
who longed " to depart and be with Christ," [3] told them
to show themselves "guileless and above reproach,
faultless children of God in a warped and crooked
generation," [4] reminded them that " we laid down the
rule: the man who will not work shall not eat," [5] and,
in spite of his longing " to depart," said, " This indeed
I know for certain: I shall stay and stand by you all to
help you forward." [6]

We have postponed till now one very important
question about the Kingdom of God because it is so
closely connected with the doing of his will on earth.
What is the relation between the Kingdom and the
Church? Are they identical? The answer is, certainly
not.

The Kingdom is a rule, an influence to which men
submit. . . . Its influence extends to all their doings,
not merely their specifically religious ones. It brings
a new life, a new hope, a new power into all their
activities, whether of work or leisure. We speak sometimes by analogy of baptizing cultures and civilisations into Christ. And that means submitting them
to the influence of Christian morals and ideals. Thus
the Kingdom is spread. But that does not necessarily enlarge the borders of the Church, for the

[1] Matthew 5 : 19.
[2] Philippians 3 : 21.
[3] Philippians 1 : 23.
[4] Philippians 2 : 14, 15.
[5] II Thessalonians 3 : 10.
[6] Philippians 1 : 25.

I

Church is the Body of Christ, and the only objects that can become limbs of his body are persons.[1]

What then is the Church? " The Church is, so to speak, the midwife that attends upon the continuous birth of the Kingdom. . . . The Church does not create the Kingdom. The new life can only come from God out of heaven. It is an eruption of supernatural power bringing the qualities of eternity into space and time." [2] Bishop Wand goes further and to " the awkward question " whether a person can be a member of the Kingdom and not of the Church, he gives the answer as "probably in the affirmative." Jesus warned the religious leaders that " many will come from east and west " to feast in the Kingdom, " but those who were born to the Kingdom will be driven out into the dark." [3] " In the Church is to be found the summing up and continuation of that work (the life and death of Jesus Christ) in so far as it proceeds and extends in time. That this thesis is a true statement of fundamentals is undoubted; but to deduce from it that the Christian's only concern should be with Church history would be to return to the pietist delusion. God is to be found in his Church, his Body, if we would seek for him; but it would be blasphemous to deny that he is at work outside his Church as well as within it." [4]

The Church, then, is never an end in itself, but God's instrument for bringing in his Kingdom; it is a body of faithful people striving to see that his will is done in earth as it is in heaven. The Lord's command was, " Go forth and make all nations my disciples; baptize men everywhere. . . . and teach them to observe all that

[1] Wand, op. cit., p. 50.　　[2] Wand, op. cit., pp. 10, 11.
[3] Matthew 8 : 11, 12.
[4] Munby, *God and the Rich Society*, p. 13.

I have commanded you." [1] Thus the Church must always be outward-looking, not a cosy little clique turned in upon itself.

Comparatively few people living to-day have any idea of what the Church has done in the world. The Church has gone to all nations with the good news of Jesus Christ, and strangely enough it was Saul the persecutor who became Paul the first missionary and who saved Christianity from becoming a sect of Judaism and saw that Jesus was the Saviour of the whole world. From St. Paul to the present day the missionary endeavour of the Church has been consistent and world-wide. But the real measure of the influence of the Church is qualitative not quantitative. Wherever the Gospel has been taken it has given men freedom from superstition and fear and has led to a richer, fuller life, socially and culturally. In our own country, with its peculiar relationship between Church and State, our Christian heritage is deeply rooted in our character, our institutions and our laws. For example, in education the Church was the first in the field. The first Church Day School was founded at Ewell, near Oxford, in 1380; the first school dinners were served at a Church School in Exeter in 1867. The Education Act of 1944 has decreed that in all schools the day shall start with an act of worship and that Religious Instruction shall be given. The Church was the first to care for the sick and the poor. The phrase " the weak to the wall " originally had quite a different meaning from what it bears to-day. It meant that the only seating provided in churches should be given to the weak. Gradually the conscience of the nation has been schooled to regard the Social Services as the responsibility of the State and so

[1] Matthew 28 : 19.

we have our Welfare State which has taken over those
services which formerly were left to the Church and
voluntary charitable organisations. Happily we are still
rich in voluntary societies which work side by side with
State and Local Government and help to fill in the gaps
in the Welfare State. Behind the Labour Party, and,
indeed, the inspiration of it, lies a long line of Christian
Socialists; and history records the lead given in all
reforms by Christian men and women—John Colet, John
Howard, William Wilberforce, Elizabeth Fry, Lord
Shaftesbury, Florence Nightingale, William Temple, and
so on. Indeed, the political and social influence of
Christian people played no small part in saving our
country from revolution at a time when revolutions were
taking place all over Europe.

It has often been shown by historians how Noncon-
formity, more than any other fact, prevented the
most disastrous consequences of the division into
" two nations " (dramatised by Disraeli's novel
Sybil in 1845) by providing its own outlet for the
energies of the rising classes through the chapel
system, and by providing, too, an example to
Chartists and others of law-abiding dissent. . . .
G. D. H. Cole and Raymond Postgate . . . join the
radical dissenting ministers with the mainly Anglican
" Christian Socialists," and observe of them that
" they were responsible for preventing that hostility
between the organised working class and organised
religion which became universal on the Continent.
There was, henceforward, always a small percentage
of persons with a genuine sympathy with socialism
and the misery of the working class, whose influence

prevented the Church and the Chapels being counted wholly as enemies: similarly a strain of religiosity and pietism ran powerfully in the Labour movement and was later to be an effective obstacle to the spread of Marxian philosophy." [1]

Even to-day

the living Church, though never neat, keeps God's world from complete disaster. . . . Do not forget that the present Church, as it is with all its praise and blame, is out and away the most active community in our land. Compared with those active in all the political parties put together, the Church's active membership is as one hundred to one. It has a record of weekly attendance that no trades union or trade association can begin to approximate.[2]

All this, and much more, is unknown to the vast majority of people. They do not know that the lot is fallen unto them in fair ground, that they have a goodly heritage. They are enjoying its fruits and pulling up the roots, or to put it another way, living on the capital stored up in the past. A visit to a country which has no such heritage or where that heritage is being "educated" out of the life of the people would open their eyes. Many things which we take for granted, many of the values, on which we live without a thought for their origin, do not exist. We should be faced literally with a different kind of life. Thus there are thousands to-day to whom religion, let alone the Church, is irrelevant to

[1] Daniel Jenkins, *Equality and Excellence*, pp. 211, 212, in the chapter, "Equality as part of our Heritage," by David L. Edwards.
[2] George MacLeod, *Only One Way Left*, p. 94.

their lives.   Their attitude might be described in a parody of a well-known hymn:

> To every man the castle
> Is handed on a plate.
> Their creed is " science teaches ",
> Their God the Welfare State.

They do not need the Church to dispense " charity ", sin is either rationalised or not in their vocabulary at all, they are doubtful whether the human personality survives death, and if there is no such thing as sin or eternity, judgment is not worth bothering about, for if it comes at all, it must come in this world and in this world the sinner, if he is a sinner, often seems to come off quite well.[1]

Who is to blame, these people or the Church? We cannot, we dare not, apportion blame.   But Jesus did say that God's will must be done on earth and he did give his Church this commission.   And we must never forget that any failures of the Church are the failures of Christians.   The Church has done much, very much, on earth, but we can never be complacent and rest on past achievements.   Our duty lies with the present and the future and we must face it.   One of the speakers at the World Council of Churches Assembly at New Delhi in December 1961 said, " There was a madman who lived among the tombs of the dead.   He was where many men still are, still wedded to a world that has passed away, still clinging to tasks that have become outmoded, still nostalgically murmuring the slogans of forgotten years." [2]

[1] See *Christian Education Reviewed*, Spencer Leeson, pp. 63, 64, on " the great omission "—the judgment of the righteous God on Sin.
 [2] Dr. D. T. Niles.

The writer was once sitting in the congregation at a service and overheard this conversation between two small boys. " Have you been to church before? " " No!" " Have you been to the British Museum? " We have already seen that we might have been spared some of the dangerous substitutes for the Kingdom from which the world has suffered had there been a clearer doctrine of the Kingdom and Christians faithful to it. But sometimes the Church seems to be more occupied with itself than with the Kingdom of God.

The primary concern of Christians is with people, and since human institutions and governments are concerned with people we must not belittle their importance which would be tantamount to thinking that they are incapable, or in no need of, redemption. All these must be baptised into the Kingdom of God and, if they are not, there is the danger that institutions will become more important than the people they are meant to serve and care for. The Sabbath was made for man, not man for the Sabbath. " The point of breakdown in the world to-day, alike in its thinking, its ethics and its politics, is the elimination of the personal. . . . If these tendencies are to be reversed, if men are again to become something more than statistical units in a mass-collectivism, the principle to which all our endeavours must now be geared is the ' Primacy of the Personal.' " [1] Mumford writes as a humanist. He sees the danger, but it is for Christians to give the answer. But the Church itself is becoming statistically minded. The figures and facts which it publishes are useful in many ways. But the danger is there. We count heads and make comparisons.

[1] Mumford, *The Condition of Man*, p. 393, quoted by Barry, *Recovery of Man*, p. 78.

We struggle to get people " into the Church." This should mean first making them our friends, and then training them in worship, in Christian living, in responsibility and leadership. But are we doing this? Does membership in the Church become an end in itself, or does it make the members responsible citizens in every sphere of life and the Church the responsible society, the salt, the leaven, the light *in the world* ?

The world is a very troublesome world, and for that very reason the Church has to be immersed in it as Jesus was, to be the Church militant here on earth.

There are no specifically religious concerns (though of course the worship of God involves particular buildings, particular ceremonies, particular people, and particular times set aside for prayer, public worship and so on). The religious man is not a man who does one thing rather than another; for example a teacher rather than industrial manager, or a tennis player rather than a football watcher. There are no concerns more particularly Christian than others, though Christians often give the impression that they have a particular corner in gambling, drink and sex, and perhaps smoking (in some circles). But there may rightly be specific matters with which particular Christians should concern themselves, and there may, at any given time in history, be a need for Christians to concentrate on some special issue which seems especially urgent to them.[1]

There are many such issues to-day—nuclear power and the nuclear deterrent, Communism, education and especially the effects upon it of the demands of science

[1] *God and the Rich Society*, Munby, p. 178.

and technology, and the whole question of equality and its wide ramifications, to mention but a few.[1]

These issues are political concerns and the Church is often told to keep out of politics. In point of fact it cannot and never has, for if politics are concerned with government and government is concerned with people, then religion must enter politics and always has done from Amos to the present day. This does not mean that there should be Christian political parties. Fortunately our country has always steered clear of them and the reason is that Christians have been found in all parties. For instance, " It is due to him [Gore], and to men like Stanton, Dolling, Headlam and Scott Holland, that the assumption usually made on the Continent that Christianity and Socialism are incompatible has never been accepted in England." [2] There are no Christian political programmes and no cut and dried answers to political, economic and social problems, but there are Christian principles and standards which must be applied to them. The trouble comes when there are not enough Christians in politics to voice these principles, to draw together people of different shades of opinion and to lessen partisanship and acrimony. We may well ask ourselves whether we are not suffering to-day from this deficiency and whether the laity are sufficiently reminded that for some of them their " church work " may lie in state or local government politics rather than in parochial duties. This is especially applicable to the younger generation who must succeed the older stalwarts who have given their time and talents to this Christian Service.

[1] See especially *Equality and Excellence*, Daniel Jenkins.
[2] *The Christian in Politics*, Walker James, p. 115. This book is an interesting study of the whole subject.

Behind and in support of all this lies the need of theologians who will help us to apply the eternal message of the Gospel to contemporary problems. There is a dearth of social theology. In consequence, the theology of the Church gives the impression of being backward-looking. In a sense it must be so, for it is founded on the life of Jesus who lived in a world very different from our own. But we cannot imprison Jesus in his own age. It is significant that when Christmas comes round people delight to worship the Babe in the Crib, forgetting that he did not stay there, but grew up to man's estate. And yet the Christmas hymn tells us what we have to do:

> Trace we the Babe, who hath retrieved our loss,
> From his poor manger to his bitter cross;
> Tread in his steps, assisted by his grace,
> Until man's first heavenly state again takes place.

Because Jesus is the same yesterday, to-day and for ever, he is the only true contemporary, and his Body, the Church, must be so too. This need for a contemporary theology is extremely difficult to fulfil. The function of the Church is to preserve the teaching and traditions entrusted to it. There is no new Gospel, and, we may add, no new morality. But the Church must not give the impression of being timid, lacking in the spirit of adventure, hesitant to speak out boldly. It must not shrink from giving offence if it is to challenge indifference and outworn ideas. On the other hand it has to try to express its theology in such a way that it will not endanger, let alone destroy, the faith of good, simple folk or leave them in bewilderment. Moreover it has to face the fact that newspapers, wireless and television have an enormous impact on millions of people and are shaping their

thinking and their outlook on life. Thus the task before
the Church is as difficult as the need is great. For

> the important question, and it is one which many
> people quite understandably shrink from considering,
> is whether the same presentation which chimed with
> the needs of men two thousand years ago, in their
> then circumstances, can effectively impart the same
> unchanging truths now. . . . The manner in which
> unchanging Christian truths are expressed needs the
> most careful examination in relation to the state of
> human knowledge. It is the manner in which they
> are expressed that must be made contemporary if
> the unchanging truths are to be kept alive and to
> gain acceptance. It would not be wrong to say that
> this problem requires the kind of theological scholar-
> ship which is at present not very actively pursued and
> that the need for it grows day by day and year by
> year more important.[1]

There is a similar, if not a more urgent need, for a
revision of our services. We cannot expect people to
know and do the will of God unless their instinctive need
to worship is satisfied. But if we do get people to Church,
the services will be largely meaningless, and sometimes
actually repellent, to anyone not brought up on the
Bible and the Prayer Book, and perhaps to some who are.
Can we really retain such phrases in the collects as " God
who madest infants to glorify thee by their death " or
" grant us the true circumcision of the Spirit "? Some
of the Old Testament lessons are unintelligible without
a commentary and some of the psalms are full of complacent self-righteousness and are bloodthirsty and un-

[1] *Christianity and the World Today*, Philip Morris, pp. 148, 151.

christian. Of course all these have a meaning and a message, but they do not speak simply and clearly without explanation. No doubt the Prayer Book safeguards the laity from the idiosyncrasies of the clergy and sets a pattern of worship in which there is atmosphere, beauty and symbolism. But how can the uninitiated catch this without preliminary training with simpler and more intelligible forms of worship? The clergy are handicapped in their work. Those who are responsible for teaching children and young people should not continually have to say, "Of course this doesn't mean literally what it says; the real meaning is. . . ." It is to the credit of the clergy that, handicapped as they are, so many of them manage to lead simple, dignified and intelligible acts of worship which cannot fail to make their appeal.

There are two other handicaps under which the clergy labour—the extreme conservatism of many of the laity and the shortage in the ministry. Many a vicar sees the need for changes and new methods, but is continually baulked by his Church Council and " the faithful." They may be few in number, but they have "possessed" their church for years. They are selfish and blind to the mission of the Church. Their motto is " as it was in the beginning is now and ever shall be." As for the ministry, the last Lambeth Report said that it is of little use to discuss the future of the Anglican Communion unless we can guarantee a ministry sufficient in number and quality to serve the expanding mission of the Church. But what use to talk of " expanding mission " when the annual number of men ordained hardly equals the wastage through death and retirement, let alone makes up the large deficit that already exists? And if we remember that the ministry is one total ministry in which clergy and laity share, we must learn how to offer more opportunities to the laity than are open to them at present. This is particularly urgent in connection with lay women.

We have said enough to show that there is no room for complacency. But it is equally true that pessimism would be quite wrong. We have never had a more devoted and hard-working body of clergy. The laity are becoming more articulate and claiming their rightful place in the Church. In every parish there are to be found committed laymen and laywomen who are the salt of the earth. Christian Stewardship is slowly becoming a recognised feature of parish life, and is teaching us that we are God's stewards for everything he has given us to use. Some bold spirits, clerical and lay, are making experiments and finding them amazingly successful. The Church is beginning to learn the need for extra-parochial ministries. There are manifest signs of life and movement. The Church is alive and always will be because Christ is alive in his Body.

" The wind blows where it wills; you hear the sound of it, but you do not know where it comes from, or where it is going." [1] The wind of the Spirit is blowing through the Church to-day. We do not yet know where it will lead us; but the real question is whether we are willing to be led. Jesus was led by the Spirit and he obeyed. He lived the prayer he taught us and lived it in the world which is his own. But the world " did not recognise him. He entered his own realm, and his own would not receive him." [2] That tragedy has been repeated in the history of the Church; it must not be our sad story. Our prayer that his will may be done on earth will be

[1] John 3 : 8.   [2] John 1 : 11.

empty unless we hear and obey what the spirit is saying to the Church to-day. " Today if you will hear his voice, harden not your hearts." [1]

When Jesus followed " thy Kingdom come " with " thy will be done " he was not only telling us how the Kingdom would come but also that we have the obligation and the privilege to work for it. *He* inaugurated it, *he* alone established it, nothing in the end can thwart *his* will; but he does work in and through us. Here then is a doctrine of ministry and it is one total ministry. There are different functions but all of us, clergy and laity alike, must share in it, for we are all " consecrated by the Spirit so as to be obedient to Jesus Christ." [2]

Secondly, there is a doctrine of the Church. The Church is not the Kingdom, but God's agent for bringing it into the world. Thus the Church is never an end in itself, but must be ever outward-looking, seeking to add to the membership of the Kingdom. This it will never be if the function of its ministry is seen simply as "getting people into the Church." Another name for total ministry is Christian Stewardship, and only when we understand what that means will the Church be faithful to its trust.

Thirdly, " in earth " once again reminds us of the meaning of the Incarnation. Jesus is always contemporary with his world, the only true contemporary, and he calls on his Church to be contemporary with her Lord.

Lastly, if we can speak of a doctrine of the will of God, it is a doctrine of the adventure of faith, a faith always ready to launch out into the deep. There are guides and disciplines which will help us to learn the will of

[1] Psalm 95.   [2] Wand's translation of I Peter 1 : 2.

God—the word of God in the Bible, the life and teaching of Jesus, the authority and experience of the Church. All these we need to educate and enlighten our conscience and to check any presumptuous claim to infallible personal guidance. But behind them all is the indispensable doctrine of the Spirit of Truth. This Holy Spirit, though truly the " Comforter " who makes us strong, gives us the least comfortable of all Christian doctrines. He is symbolised by wind and fire; we never know whither he will lead us or with what he will set our hearts aflame. But we do know that he is the Spirit of Jesus, our King and our Lord, the Way, the Truth and Life. Through him we shall not only perceive and know what things we ought to do, but also gain courage and power to be faithful stewards of the Kingdom of God.

VII. GIVE US THIS DAY
OUR DAILY BREAD

Is there a man among you who will offer his son a stone when he asks for bread, or a snake when he asks for fish? If you, then, bad as you are, know how to give your children what is good for them, how much more will your heavenly Father give good things to them who ask him!

Matthew 7 : 9-11

Bread for myself is a material problem; bread for other people is a spiritual problem.

Nicolas Berdyaev

Our wealth is overwhelming; only let us be careful that it does not overwhelm us!

D. L. Munby, *God and the Rich Society*, p. 174

Dean Inge once said, the bored people are those who are consuming much, but producing little.

Leslie Davison, *Preacher's Gold*, p. 44

TO SAY that this is the first prayer for ourselves in the Lord's Prayer is not strictly correct because to reverence God's name, to work for the extension of his Kingdom and to do his will must affect our lives. It really is true that his service is perfect freedom. But here is a petition for our own physical needs, and it immediately poses the question—may we pray for things? And if we may, on what conditions?

The first answer is perfectly simple; Jesus gave us the prayer and that is that. The conditions cannot be described so shortly or so simply. There are two—we can pray for things provided that to have them will serve God's will; and we must pray as a family. We ask " Give us ", not " give me ". There will be a good deal to say about the second later on. As to the first, all that has already been said about God's will must apply in petitionary prayer. In the agony in Gethsemane Jesus prayed that he might not be killed. " Father, if it be thy will, take this cup away from me. Yet not my will but thine be done." [1] When the mother of Zebedee's sons asked for the first places for them in the Kingdom, Jesus said, " You do not understand what you are asking. Can you drink the cup that I am to drink? " [2] Did they know what the request involved? Were they prepared to pay the price? Often we do not understand what we are asking. It is rather like that macabre play, *The Monkey's Paw*, in which a man and his wife have a paw which will give them the fulfilment of three wishes. By the first wish they get a sum of money but it is in compensation for the death of their son who met his death by accident in a factory. With the second they wish him alive again, only to realise that he may appear crippled and torn by the machinery which caused his death. Just in time they use the third to wish him dead again and at peace. But there is a difference between this story and prayer. God can and does say No and thereby saves us many a time from the consequences of unwise petitions. We may grumble and say that our prayer is not answered. The truth is that every prayer is answered. The answer may be No, and if we could see all and understand all, as God does, we should be thankful that he has said No. But as our knowledge is only partial, we have to trust

[1] Luke 22 : 42.   [2] Matthew 20 : 22.

God. " Father knows best " is an irritating reply to a child, but the Christian who prays " Our Father " ought not to be so childish as to think that God will spoil him. He loves us too much. Parents who spoil their children do not love their children enough to say No; they will not cause them immediate sorrow and annoyance for their future good.

But why must we pray at all if God is our Father and wants us to have what is good for us? The answer lies in our freedom. The need for prayer, and the instinct to pray, are a very valuable proof of that freedom and God's respect for it. We have to work and we have to pray and both must be creative co-operation with the will of God. It is easier to see that we have to work because God's gifts have to be used and applied. Hence the phrase " working is praying ". So it is, but it sometimes becomes an excuse for praying too little or not at all. Prayer is the expression of our dominant desires and our chief desire should be that whatever we ask for may be in accordance with God's will. If our petitions are made in this spirit, we shall be able to avoid some mistakes. One is what we may bluntly call " silly prayers ". A girl prays that she may pass an exam when she has not done enough work to make it possible. A man asks to be delivered from a certain sin when he does not take the trouble to avoid the occasions which lead to it. A gambler prays that his " luck " may be in, when the odds against him are astronomical. This kind of prayer is an offence against reason. It turns prayer into magic and God into a magician. It is also an offence against our freedom, for it asks God to overrule our freedom and our co-operation with him. Then there are the " last resort prayers ". Shakespeare gives some

examples of these. " All's lost! To prayers, to prayers." [1]
" Now I, to comfort him, bid him 'a should not think of
God; I hoped there was no need to trouble himself
with any such thoughts yet." [2] Some of us know that
when a clergyman has suggested prayers in church for a
sick person he has received the reply, " He's not that bad
yet." (Invariably from relatives, not from the patient,
and happily not so common to-day.) These prayers are
not wrong, for nothing is more natural than prayer
when we are in great difficulty or fear. The mistake is
in using prayer only as a last resort, as if God comes in
only when things have got beyond human control. If
we are in the habit of praying when life is serene, we shall
the more easily turn to God when sorrow and pain
come.

Then there are " problem prayers ". Recently some
sixth-form boys from a Grammar School were putting
questions to a panel of three men. One of the questions
was, " May we pray for victory in a war? " The answer
given was, " Yes, if it is a just war." Thus in the last
war, if we were sure that we were fighting for the freedom
of the world, we could pray for victory. But that opens
up the large question—what is a just war? And what if
—as is certainly bound to be the case—both sides are
praying for victory? Or, to turn to more domestic
affairs, may we pray that someone we love may not die
or be killed, that the holiday we are looking forward to
may not be spoilt by rain, that we may be promoted to
a post which will make life easier for wife and family?
These are puzzles which we cannot solve because we
are not omniscient. But surely we shall not be wrong
to pray for victory, for the safety of those we love, for

[1] *The Tempest.*   [2] *Henry V.*

innocent pleasures and comforts for our families, provided that we can not only add, " yet not my will but thine be done," but also accept disappointment and sorrow in this spirit. And we can take a hint from the father who said that he would rather his boy prayed " Please God, make Daddy brave " than " Please God, keep Daddy safe." [1]

Jesus said, " Man cannot live on bread alone," [2] he never said that man has no need of bread; and in this clause he recognises our stark, physical needs. We know we cannot ignore them and he tells us not to. William Temple said that Christianity is the most materialistic of all religions. That means that in Christianity there is a synthesis between the spiritual and material. Both make demands upon us, demands which we often find it hard to reconcile. Hence the temptation to solve the problem by escaping from and ignoring the one or the other. A man's religion becomes either world-renouncing or world-affirming. If he adopts the former, he will contract out of the calls and the duties of life in the world. He may even be led to extravagant lengths of asceticism to escape from the demands of his physical body. If his religion becomes world-affirming, he will tend to become a humanist, and his religion will become more and more secular and " welfare " will become simply material. Teilhard de Chardin writes of " the Problem of the two Energies " and

the dynamic relationships which exist between the *within* and the *without* of things. . . . We are perfectly aware in our concrete actions that the two opposite forces combine. The motor works, but we cannot

[1] Studdert Kennedy.   [2] Matthew 4 : 4.

make out the method, which seems to be contradictory . . . our action seems at once to depend on, and
yet to be independent of, material forces. First of
all, the dependence. This is depressingly and
magnificently obvious. " To think, we must eat."
That blunt statement expresses a whole economy,
and reveals, according to the way we look at it, either
the tyranny of matter or its spiritual power. The
loftiest speculation, the most burning love, are, as
we know only too well, accompanied and paid for
by an expenditure of physical energy. Sometimes
we need bread, sometimes wine, sometimes a tonic
or a hormone injection, sometimes the stimulation of
a colour, sometimes the magic of a sound which goes
in at our ears as a vibration and teaches our brains
in the form of inspiration. Without the slightest
doubt there is *something* through which material and
spiritual energy hold together and are complementary.[1]

Here we have the problem of the Phenomenon of Man.
And although it would be foolish and impossible to
attempt to try to follow the argument of this great book
in a few words, we can at least see from this quotation
the problem with which it is concerned. Man cannot
live by bread alone, but he must have bread. Man is
both material and spiritual. And this is precisely what
Jesus was. God in Jesus was made man to show us that
all life is sacramental. The material cannot and must
not be ignored. But the material only finds its true
function and meaning when its spiritual significance is
seen. Bread for myself is not solely a material problem;

[1] *The Phenomenon of Man,* p. 63.

nor is bread for other people solely a spiritual problem; for to think, I must eat, and the satisfaction of my own material needs is not an end in itself, but a means through which my spiritual powers can be used. The synthesis between the spiritual and the material is to be found in Jesus Christ who is *the* Sacrament, the Sacrament of God. All other sacraments, and all life lived sacramentally, depend on him. This is " exemplified in the sacramental system of his church and particularly in the Eucharist. The natural bread and wine, won by the combined labour of man and the abundant blessing of the Father, are taken and made the Body and the Blood of the Son, and, becoming part of the person of the worshipper, assist in his spiritual transformation until body and soul alike receive their fulfilment in the ocean of God's love." [1]

" The combined labour of man and the abundant blessing of the Father "— man and Providence. But just how much is due to man and how much to Providence? The nearer we are to nature the easier it is to see the hand of Providence. " A man scatters seed on the land; he goes to bed at night and gets up in the morning, and the seed sprouts and grows—how, he does not know. The ground produces a crop by itself." [2] But every farmer knows that it will be a poor crop unless he ploughs, harrows, fertilises and weeds. And then the weather and the hand of Providence again. With the advance of science still more and more seems to be due to man, less and less to Providence. There was a time when all that happened was attributed to the Providence of God. As knowledge has increased it has become less fashionable to attribute to God what are regarded as

[1] Wand, *The Mystery of the Kingdom*, p. 86.   [2] Mark 4 : 26–8.

normal and everyday events. Thus it has become more
and more difficult to think of the Providence of God.
" Both the ' scientific attitude ' and the implicit ideas in
social revolution, can create and fortify the assumption
that with knowledge and power men can make their own
world—and that they alone must make it." [1]

The answer to this situation is to know what the
Providence of God really means. If we think of God as
a kind of universal provider and we now think of the
Welfare State in the same way, then naturally the
Welfare State will take the place of God. This attitude
is, of course, wrong in both cases. God never has handed
things to us in this way. All his gifts are dependent
upon man's ability to use them and his willingness to
work. Similarly, as we have already said, the Welfare
State is bound to break down unless we are prepared to
take our share in the whole economy of the nation by
work of brain and hand. God has given us the freedom
of responsibility in the use of his gifts. The Welfare
State is no substitute for that; indeed it demands a very
high sense of responsibility and interdependence and a
very highly developed sense of community.

There is a further consideration. Nothing that man
has achieved by skill and science has ever altered the
fact that he cannot make the raw materials on which he
lives and which he uses in such wonderful ways. He
produces steam but does not make coal, he uses elec-
tricity but he does not make it, he grows penicillin but he
does not make the culture, he produces paper but he
does not make the tree which makes the wood which
makes the pulp which is turned into paper. Professor

[1] Bishop E. R. Wickham quoted in Munby's *God and the Rich
Society*, p. 15. See also pp. 13–16.

Coulson tells us [1] that the first half of the twentieth century will be known as the period in world history when men first acquired almost unlimited control over the physical forces of nature—and then they will go on to say, " But it was only just in time." Half the coal ever used has been consumed in the last twenty-five years, and half the oil in the last ten years. If the underdeveloped countries acquire an industrial life and if the population of the world continues to increase as it is now doing, where will all the power needed come from? Just in time comes atomic energy. It is not new in the sense that it was not there before; its discovery and its use are new and are due to the amazing skill and ingenuity of man.

By what conceivable process of reasoning can we exclude from God's providence the skill and ingenuity of man? We have a right to speak of the wonderful works of man, but only if we see that man himself is a creature of God, that only God gives life and with life the ever-widening reach of man's brain and hand and eye. " God moves in a mysterious way his wonders to perform," but those wonders are to be seen not only in nature but in man's mastery of nature. The strongest argument for the Providence of God is man himself.

> Lift every gift that thou thyself hast given;
> Low lies the best till lifted up to heaven:
> Low lie the bounding heart, the teeming brain,
> Till, sent from God, they mount to God again.[2]

We can do three things with the gifts of God: we can

---

[1] *Some Problems of the Atomic Age*, pp. 10, 11.
[2] H. M. Butler, *English Hymnal*, No. 429.

abuse them, or not-use them, or use them. Abuse leads
to disaster. The obvious example is the misapplication
of nuclear energy in the bomb. To turn that source of
energy, which has come to us only just in time, to de-
structive ends is the judgment we pass on ourselves.
And again there appears this dangerous, but inescapable,
gift of freedom. We are free to choose. Secondly, we
can not-use them. It is illuminating how often in the
New Testament the sin of not-doing appears and is
condemned. The Kingdom of Heaven

> is like a man going abroad, who called his servants
> and put his capital in their hands ... The man who
> had been given one bag [of gold] came and said ...
> " Master, ... I was afraid, and I went and hid your
> gold in the ground. Here it is—you have what
> belongs to you." " You lazy rascal! " said the
> master. ... " Take the bag of gold from him, and
> give it to the one who has ten bags. For the man
> who has will always be given more, till he has
> enough and to spare; and the man who has not will
> forfeit even what he has."[1]

So also were condemned Dives who never even noticed
the beggar at his gates, the foolish women who never
bothered to fill their lamps with oil, and, above all, those
who did nothing to feed the hungry, clothe the naked and
visit the prisoners. " I was afraid." Yes, we may well
be, for the gifts of God are two-edged, a blessing or a
curse; and sometimes we wish they had never been
discovered. But it is no good, we cannot put the clock
back. We are faced with a great challenge and it would
seem that God is trusting us to-day as people have never

[1] Matthew 25 : 14 ff.

been trusted before. And the one thing we cannot do is to do nothing.

To use God's gifts means to use them as he intends them to be used. " Low lie the bounding heart, the teeming brain " until they are in his service. A corollorary of the doctrine of Providence is the doctrine of work. Jesus said, " My Father has never yet ceased his work, and I am working too." [1] God's creative activity is not finished, it is still going on, and we are meant to share in it. It is easy enough to say the obvious things on what this means. Every man has a duty to work. St. Paul put this very bluntly, " During our stay with you we laid down the rule: the man who will not work shall not eat. We mention this because we hear that some of your number are idling their time away, minding everybody's business but their own." [2] And although he was dealing with a situation that had arisen because of the expectation of an early return of our Lord, he would probably not have objected to a general application of his rule. Every man should approach his work with a sense of vocation, for that word is not the perquisite of a few privileged occupations—in spite of the Inland Revenue phrase, " trade, profession or calling " —but ought to be applicable to all work, and we can hardly hope to see the doctrine of work in practice until it can be and is so applied. Then again every man ought to see his work, not simply as a means of earning a living, but as a service to the community. Man cannot live by bread alone. Thus he should find satisfaction in his work. Finally, he ought to see his work as creative because he is sharing in the creative work of God. These things probably need saying, however obvious and

[1] John 5 : 17.   [2] II Thessalonians 3 : 10, 11.

familiar they may be; for there is no doubt that there
is a good deal of lazy, dishonest and shoddy work about.
" One hears a good deal about the first part [of the fourth
commandment]—keeping the Sabbath holy—but a great
deal less, if anything at all, about the second—that in
six days one should do all one has to do." [1] There is some
tendency to expect more and more to be " laid on "
in the form of state subsidies until wages are regarded
as pocket money for leisure spending. Then there are
the attractive inducements not to work of the huge prizes
offered by the pools and other gambling facilities—
facilities which the Government extended and parti-
cipated in, with the relaxation of the betting laws and the
introduction of Premium Bonds, at the same time as they
were telling us that nothing but hard work would set our
country on its feet.

But when all these obvious things have been said it is
equally obvious that we have not formulated a Christian
doctrine of work. A man has not only a duty, but also
a right, to work. His work should be a vocation, but
can it always be so? How far can he choose the work
that he will do? Can he always see his work as a service
to the community, does he always know exactly what
part he is playing in a complicated industrial process?
Is it to be wondered at that a man seeks relief from the
boredom and drudgery of many kinds of work in gambling
and the like? " Blessed be drudgery " is the cliché of
those who know not drudgery. These are only some of
the questions we have to ask ourselves. Underlying them
are complex economic problems. What, for instance,
are we to say of an economy which involves the employ-
ment on a large scale of married women and mothers?

[1] Sir A. fforde, *The Times*, 15th July, 1958.

The emancipation of women has established their right to a career, but have we made any attempt to assess the effect on home and family life? Have people a right to strike, and if so, who have this right and when? Lord Fisher of Lambeth was reported to have said that no man has the right to strike for money unless he is starving. It was left to a young priest-workman to challenge this statement and to point out that to strike means to withhold labour; and that just as a man may decline to sell his goods unless he gets a fair price for them, so the worker who has only his labour to sell may decline to work.

It is clear that we need people who will study these complicated issues and give us guidance on them. There is a great dearth of theologians who understand the economic and social patterns of this day and age and work out therefrom a Christian doctrine of work.[1] Meantime the Christian has to do the best he can as an individual and in society. He can set a high standard of industry and integrity. As employer or employee he can try to cultivate proper personal relations with his fellows. He can try to maintain the dignity of work by his attitude to his own work and his respect for the work of others. But above all he can try to uphold the principle of the dignity of man, which means that man is more important than the machine, by fighting every tendency to depersonalise man. For behind the doctrine of work lies the doctrine of man himself. " More than a century ago, Frederick Denison Maurice remarked that the modern world seems to be producing a kind of man to whom the Christian gospel cannot be preached. . . . The primary task of the evangelist is not to recover indus-

[1] One recent notable exception is *Equality and Excellence* by Daniel Jenkins.

trialised man for God and the Church, but rather to recover him for himself. The masses must become men again if they are to hear God speak." [1] The same need is expressed from a different angle in a Penguin Special with the ominous title *The Stagnant Society*.[2] The author points out that strikes frequently occur " as a result of simple muddle and misunderstanding. The ease with which this can happen is itself evidence of the gaps in communication which still exist in our society, and the strength of surviving suspicions."

Men must have bread, but how much? and how is it to be determined what is enough? Jesus said, " Give us this day our daily bread," and that means enough for our daily needs. The word " daily " is important because it is easy enough to forget that we cannot live by bread alone and " cannot serve God and Money. Therefore I bid you put away anxious thoughts about food and drink to keep you alive, and clothes to cover your body." God looks after the lilies and the grass and the birds and he will look after you. " Do not be anxious about to-morrow; to-morrow will look after itself." [3] No one will imagine that this is an invitation to improvidence. It is the point where the doctrine of work and the doctrine of Providence meet. We are to work for our daily needs, but if we work to store up treasure on earth, we shall run into serious trouble; for " where your wealth is, there will your heart be also." [4]

Here we are up against the same need to examine the Christian life in the present situation. We live in " the affluent society ". One aim predominates—in-

---

[1] Langmead Casserley, *The Retreat from Christianity*, p. 122, 3.
[2] By Michael Shanks, published 1961, p. 63 *passim*.
[3] Matthew 6 : 24 ff.   [4] Matthew 6 : 21.

creasingly to control environment to improve the material conditions of life and to gain a greater physical and material security. *And it is not wrong.* Why should it be? God gives us his gifts to use and enjoy. But there are plenty of other things to consider as well. There are things of importance to man besides the material and physical, and in the pursuit of the latter he will find himself face to face with questions about personal relations, social justice, fair shares, equality of opportunity and so on. He is in fact faced with the question of values and priorities. Secondly, he will have to decide when enough is enough. We all know about " keeping up with the Joneses " and the shocking " never had it so good " election slogan. Envy and greed are among the deadly sins and none of us is entirely innocent. But " the more prosperous among us do well to remember that the vast majority of the inhabitants of these islands, even when they are in work, are not yet so wealthy that they are in danger of being corrupted and corroded by their wealth." [1] Daily bread does not mean luxury, still less luxury for some and poverty for others. Thirdly, we have to welcome the Welfare State as an experiment which makes great demands on moral character, for it depends on mutual responsibility and a society in which each cares for all and all for each, and no one can attain to that degree of unselfish love and dedication without the grace of God.

Thus for the Christian there are principles to guide him. Simplicity of life which does not continually create more wants, consideration of the true values so that the standard of living does not jeopardise the standards of life, a constant watch against envy, greed and sloth in

[1] *Equality and Excellence*, p. 92.

himself, and, above all, constant consideration of others as well as of himself—these are some of the things which will help him to enjoy his daily bread.

All this leads up to the principle of sharing. Give *us*. No part of the Lord's prayer can we pray in the singular, and this clause least of all. The report of the last Lambeth Conference has a great deal to say about this. " With nations, as with individuals, the ultimate hypocrisy of the rich is to preach the virtue of poverty to the poor." To help the underdeveloped countries of the world there is needed £1000 million a year. Britain's share of this would be £150 million a year, and " this would postpone by less than a year the expected rise of 50 per cent in British living standards over the next quarter of a century." [1] The infant mortality rate in Britain is 26.5 per thousand; in India about 200.[2] Dr. George MacLeod asks the question, " What if we have ' exported our proletariat'? What if Africa and South East Asia now, by their ill-paid sweat, make rich the Western world? " [3] The expectation of life at birth for both sexes varies between 71 in Great Britain and 35 in India.[4] The world population increases at the rate of about 90,000 a day.

Medicine and every social philosophy based on the sacredness of human life and personality conspire to save life where it can be saved, and to preserve it and enrich it to the limit of possibility. It is, therefore, the application of modern science in obedience to Christian and what we might call Hippocratic

---

[1] *The Family in Contemporary Society*, p. 10, footnote.
[2] Op. cit., p. 11.
[3] *Only One Way Left*, pp. 17, 18.
[4] *The Family in Contemporary Society*, p. 38.

ethics which has created the problem of over-population as we know it in the world today. Can we now seriously consider a halt in this endeavour? Ought we still to strive to keep more babies alive, knowing that every success brings nearer the possibility that they may face starvation and social disaster in their lifetime? [1]

The same dilemma was posed by Professor Hill, speaking as Chairman to the British Association in 1952. " If ethical principles," he said, " deny our right to do evil that good may come, are we justified in doing good when the foreseeable consequence is evil? " [2] There is even the danger that truth may be suppressed out of fear. This was the subject of Charles Morgan's play, *The Burning Glass*. But you cannot put the clock back. Man's search for truth is part of man's make-up. The dilemma is just one more example of the enormous trust God places in us and the power for good or evil which accompanies his gifts.

Power over things leads to power over people; thus scientific and technical advances can never be safe unless accompanied by a philosophy and a culture which hold that man is an end in himself and not a means to an end. It would be quite possible to carry our scientific and technical achievements to underdeveloped countries without Western culture which is based on Christianity and is still Christian at heart. Thus we have not only to share our bread with our brothers, but also the faith which tells us that bread alone will not satisfy their needs.

[1] op. cit, p. 12.
[2] Quoted by Garbett, *World Problems of Today*, p. 68. See also pp. 42, 63.

And we cannot do that if we are in danger of losing it ourselves. It is not unthinkable that God, who used Cyrus as his instrument to bring judgment on the Jews who had failed in the task given them, is to-day using Communism to bring us to our senses. " It has been said that Marxians and Humanists are asking the right questions but giving false answers, while Christians, who know the true answers, have not yet learnt to ask the right questions." [1] This is true enough; it is also true that the sooner we stop talking about problems and speak of opportunities the better.

Basically our duty is quite plain; it is the principle of sharing. " If a man has enough to live on, and yet when he sees his brother in need shuts up his heart against him, how can it be said that the divine love dwells in him? " " We for our part have crossed over from death to life; this we know, because we love our brothers." [2] Jesus said quite explicitly that our salvation depends on whether we feed the hungry, clothe the naked and care for the prisoners.[3] And, says Dr. MacLeod, "perhaps the most disturbing element about that parable is the explicit assurance that neither those saved nor those condemned had any conception that they were dealing with a religious issue at all. ' Lord, when saw we thee anhungered?' " [4]

Be sure you act on the message and do not merely listen; for that would be to mislead yourselves. A man who listens to the message but never acts upon it is like one who looks in the mirror at the face nature gave him. He glances at himself and goes away, and at once forgets what he looked like. But the man

[1] Barry, *Recovery of Man*, p. 56.
[2] I John 3 : 14, 17.   [3] Matthew 25 : 31 ff.
[4] *Only One Way Left*, pp. 133, 134.

who looks closely into the perfect law, the law that makes us free, and who lives in its company, does not forget what he hears, but acts upon it; and that is the man who by acting will find happiness. [1]

Message, action, happiness—these words might well describe every clause in the Lord's Prayer, for every one of them is a message which must lead to action which will lead to happiness. This is particularly true with the clause which is the first direct petition for ourselves. First, it tells us what is the true doctrine of all prayer—to learn the will of God. Once we accept this, we can pray for anything. It is a very hard lesson because it means to desire that God's will may be done even if this involves the answer No to our own petitions. It means that we have implicit trust not only in God's omniscience but also in his love. Secondly, we find here a doctrine of things. Because God was made man in Jesus, there is no dichotomy between the spiritual and the material. We cannot and must not ignore things, but we shall never be satisfied with bread alone because we are human beings. Running right through life is the sacramental principle, that things only find their true significance when they become vehicles of spiritual realities. Thirdly, the doctrine of Providence is vindicated. " All good giving and every perfect gift comes from above, from the Father of the lights of heaven." [2] The wonderful works of man are the most important evidence of the wonderful works of God.

As for action, there is a doctrine of work and it involves rights as well as duties. And although we still await guidance on how this doctrine can be applied in the

[1] James 1 : 22-5. [2] James 1 : 17.

complex world in which we live, we can at least see some of the demands it makes upon ourselves. There is a good deal of talking which is a substitute for not doing, a good deal of waiting for a lead—" Why don't they . . . ? "—which is an excuse for inaction.

Finally, happiness. It is to be found in work which is seen as a vocation and in which there is the satisfaction of creative achievement. That this is beyond the reach of many should act as a spur to alter the conditions which rob them of this happiness. But there is a happiness within the reach of everyone and that is the happiness of sharing prompted by self-forgetful love. This in turn springs from the Christian doctrine of man which makes us see in every man a child of God and a brother of our own. This is the perfect law, the law that makes us free, for it is the law that Jesus made his own, who did not come to be served but to serve and who took a towel and washed his disciples' feet.

VIII. FORGIVE US OUR TRESPASSES AS WE FORGIVE THEM THAT TRESPASS AGAINST US

Pity is indeed the corollary of humility and repentance: you can no longer, if you have learnt the sense of sin, speak of your brother with arrogance as a sinner. We are each responsible for all. You will not say, when you see some evil done, " There but for the grace of God go I; you will say "There go I. " .... For you will know yourself implicated, responsible.

Gerald Vann, *The Divine Pity*, p. 116

While men can pass judgment on an act, it is beyond their knowledge to pass final judgment on an individual.

Kitson Clark, *The Kingdom of Free Men*, p. 173

If you go off on the other tack and proclaim that men are the helpless products of heredity and environment ... you strike a blow at the deepest and most noble of man's instincts—that is, his instinct of freedom.

Studdert Kennedy, *Lies*, p. 96

Locked up in the crucifixion were all the mysteries of God's love for the world, and of man's unspeakable ingratitude, and of God's determination, notwithstanding, to win mankind not by compulsion but by sacrifice.

Alec. R. Vidler, *Christian Belief*, p. 76

" There is mercy with thee : therefore shalt thou be feared." It is not God's anger but his mercy that breaks our hearts.

Father Andrew, *The Pattern Prayer*, p. 83

AFTER BREAD, FORGIVENESS, and we need both. It is easy enough to say we need bread for the body and forgiveness for the soul, but it is only a half-truth. Man is an indivisible personality. His physical condition may affect his whole personality and the need to be forgiven and to forgive may do so too. The superintendent of a large mental hospital said that he could discharge a large number of his patients if they could be freed from a sense of guilt. It is equally true that an unforgiving spirit may have serious reactions on mind and body.

There are three great doctrines in this clause. First, there is the fact of Sin; and let us note straight away that we mean Sin, not sins. Secondly, there is corporate Sin. Thirdly, the meaning of Forgiveness. Here we come face to face with the Cross of Jesus and of our bounden duty to forgive if we are to be forgiven. Indeed we have to face the solemn thought that we actually ask to be forgiven as we ourselves forgive; and how many of us remember this when we ask for forgiveness?

Sin is a fact. It is an attitude of rebellion, personal hostility to the will of God. It is begotten by pride and produces as unlovely offspring self-centredness, self-dependence, self-righteousness. Thus it is the exact negation of the whole teaching of the Lord's Prayer which will have nothing to do with the first person singular. Sins come from Sin which is rebellion against God, and until that is cured there is no cure for the sins. " There is no Christian solution of the problems presented by human self-will, but there is a Christian cure for the self-will, and if that is effective, the problem is (not solved but) abolished. So when a man wanted the Lord to divide an inheritance, that is to arbitrate between two self-centred claims, he refused to take that position. He will not settle the dispute; but he will tell them how

to avoid having a dispute—' Take heed and keep yourselves from all covetousness ' (St. Luke 12 : 13–16). For,
of course, if there had been no covetousness, there would
have been no dispute to settle." [1] This is exactly within
our experience when we consult the expert about our
physical or mental ills. The doctor and the psychiatrist
go behind the symptoms and tackle the root of the
trouble. Indeed, it is now freely admitted, except by
the most case-hardened atheists, that physical and mental
disorders can have a spiritual origin, in other words be
due to Sin. " Among my patients in the second half of
life," wrote Jung, " there has not been one whose
problem in the last resort was not that of finding a religious outlook on life." [2]

This attitude of rebellion can be conscious and deliberate or unconscious. The old Genesis story of the Fall
makes it quite clear that what really tempted the woman
and made her fall was the wonderful prospect of " You
will be like God ". Bertrand Russell sums up this temptation succinctly: " Every man would like to be God,
if it were possible; some few find it difficult to admit
the impossibility." [3] Very soon we find men saying,
" Come, let us build ourselves a city, and a tower with
its top in the heavens, and let us make a name for ourselves." [4] Again, equal with God. There is a striking
parallel to the Tower of Babel in Moscow. A few years
ago the writer saw the hoardings round the foundations
of the proposed Palace of the Soviets laid on the edge of
the Moscow River. A church was pulled down to make

[1] Temple, *Readings in the St. John's, Gospel* pp. 62, 63.
[2] Quoted by A. N. Gilkes in *Faith for Modern Man*, p. 59.
[3] Quoted by R. Niebuhr, *The Nature and Destiny of Man*, Vol. 1,
p. 201, note.
[4] Genesis 11 : 4.

way for it. One hears that the site has now been abandoned, but at the time the Palace was listed in *Whitaker's Almanack* as supreme amongst the " Highest Buildings in the World "—with a footnote " when completed ". To-day man's mastery of nature encourages him to dispense with God. The popular creed is " science teaches " and the popular assumption is that religion and science are incompatible. Both theologians as well as scientists are to blame for this. Unfortunately it is not yet popularly known that the wisest and humblest on both sides recognise that the assumption is quite false.

Perhaps even more dangerous than this is atheistic humanism. We have to be careful here because if we mean by a humanist one who cares greatly for the human race and reverences human beings and their achievements, there is no quarrel between Christianity and humanism. Christ himself was a humanist. But if it means, as it does to many, that man can promote his own happiness and well-being without reference to God and God's laws and without the power that comes from God, then we have described the attitude which we have called Sin. It is noteworthy that when the present Archbishop of Canterbury held his Mission to Oxford in 1960, the attack on Christianity came from those who called themselves humanists. They deplored the pessimistic view of man which Christians hold in believing in man's endemic Sin. Underlying all the questions raised at the Mission " on such things as hell and homosexuality, prayer and pacifism, dogma and divorce, was the issue of Christianity versus humanism." They were right. It is precisely this attitude, this conscious, deliberate rejection of God, which is the issue. But before we have done we shall have to see who are the real optimists.

Just how dangerous unconscious revolt from God may be is shown us in the parable of the Pharisee and the Publican. Make no mistake about it, the Pharisee was what would be called a good-living man. He went to church, he kept all the rules, and his goodness was not just negative, like the woman who said, " My husband's a good-living man, he doesn't drink and he doesn't smoke and he doesn't gamble." How many of us, even after a Christian Stewardship campaign, could say, " I give away to Church and charity a tenth part of my income"? But he had one huge fault. Everything was " I, I, I." In other words, the standard he set himself was his own, not God's. The parable " was aimed at those who were sure of their own goodness and looked down on everyone else." [1] The awful thing is that the one leads to the other. If we are *self*-satisfied, we are bound to despise others.

> Since the self judges itself by its own standards it finds itself good. It judges others by its own standards and finds them evil, when their standards fail to conform to its own. This is the secret of the relationship between cruelty and self-righteousness. When the self mistakes its standards for God's standards it is naturally inclined to attribute the very essence of evil to non-conformists. . . . The final proof that man no longer knows God is that he does not know his own sin. The sinner who justifies himself does not know God as judge and does not need God as Saviour.[2]

Whether this attitude is conscious or unconscious, it is the same thing. It either deliberately refuses to recognise

[1] Luke 18 : 9. [2] Niebuhr, op. cit., i, 212, 213.

God or is so blinded by self, pride and lust for power that it cannot see him. The result will be sins. Christianity is often accused of continually harping on sins and taking a pessimistic view of man. Part of the blame belongs to Christians themselves because they *do* harp on sins instead of keeping in the forefront the real trouble, Sin. A great deal of harm can be done by lists of questions for self-examination in some communicants' manuals, which, often long, almost wholly negative, leave one overwhelmed with many sins committed, to the exclusion of the one vital thing, the cause of them. One has even come across a manual in which so-called self-examination was not a list of questions but of statements—" I have done this and that." Even a glimmering of psychology is enough to teach us how misleading and harmful this can be. At a theological college a wise teacher said, " Examine yourself by the fruits of the Spirit rather than by the works of the devil." There is a first-rate book which does exactly this—*The Plain Man Looks at Himself*, by W. Purcell. The author says that the fruits of the Spirit are " the identification marks of the Christian." He writes on each one in turn, then gives some questions which we can ask ourselves (far more searching than the usual ones) and rounds off each " fruit " with quotations from godly men and women of all ages. A book like this can really show us how doctrine draws with it conduct in harmony with itself.

Another reason why the Christian attitude to Sin is misjudged is that it is still all too common to emphasise the sins of the flesh and neglect the far more serious envy, hatred, malice and all uncharitableness. This can easily lead to Pharisaism. If only we could show that Sin means separation from God and thus from the

source of truth, beauty and goodness, and above all from
the God who loves and inspires love, we should hear far
less about Christian pessimism. We should still hold that
sins matter and that we must never condone them, but
we should be far more concerned to get to the root of
the trouble. Christianity is both realistic and optimistic.
It faces the fact of Sin and knows that it can be cured.
Others are both unrealistic and their optimism turns out
to be an illusion. Not all the human cleverness in the
world can make one single person good. If the humanist
were right, then every advance in education, science
and knowledge would produce better men. But it does
not. We have actually seen in our own time man using
his wonderful knowledge to indulge in experiments of
cruelty which would make a decent savage blush with
shame. Now we have the power to destroy ourselves
and no one knows whether we shall do so or not. It is
useless to ask for forgiveness of sins unless we first face
the fact of Sin. That is why the first step must always be,
" I will set off and go to my father." This is conversion,
turning back home, where our Father runs to meet us
and we hear the words, " For this son of mine was dead
and has come back to life; he was lost and is found." [1]

But the parable of the Lost Son and of the Pharisee
and the Publican both illustrate the difference between
God's dealing with man and man's dealing with his
brother man. Both show us that there is corporate sin.
The Pharisee said, " I thank thee, O God, that I am not
like the rest of men, greedy, dishonest, adulterous; or,
for that matter, like this tax-gatherer." [2] The elder
brother " was angry and refused to go in." [3] Thus the
tragedy which had had a happy ending became tragedy

[1] Luke 15 : 18, 24.   [2] Luke 18 : 11.   [3] Luke 15 : 28.

again. The father found one son only to lose another. Pharisaism, pride and self-dependence lead to corporate Sin. The man who is complacently satisfied with his own rectitude ignores the fundamental principle of the Lord's Prayer, the family principle. He renounces, or is unaware of, his responsibility for others. Dr. H. Kraemer, who was Director of the Ecumenical Institute of the World Council of Churches at Bossey, shows once again how extraordinarily acute is the old Genesis story: " If the calling and aptitude toward communication in man is rooted in his right relationship to God, his Maker, Judge and Redeemer, then the distortion of communication . . . must go back to the distortion of his primal relationship. . . . Man, fallen out of his partner relationship with God, flees from God, and immediately all relationships are affected and in disorder." He puts the blame on the woman and thereby not only " practises the art of self-justification by accusing God (the woman whom *thou* gavest to be with me)", but also vitiates " the deepest of human relationships, that between man and wife. Labour, which is meant as a blessing, as partnership with God in creative activity, gets the stamp of a curse. Cain kills his brother Abel. . . . Language, the typical symbol of unity and communication amongst men, the instrument to meet each other, becomes the source of misunderstanding, disruption, and deceit." [1] How extraordinarily modern all this is, with our broken homes and " guilty parties ", our judgment of others, our deeds of violence, and all the double talk that makes communication between East and West impossible.

There are many aspects of corporate sin. Every society that punishes its anti-social members is far more

[1] *The Communication of the Christian Faith*, H. Kraemer, p. 18.

responsible for their conduct than it cares to admit. Who are the innocent, who are the guilty? Who are responsible for the broken homes, the criminal boys and girls, the deeds of lust and violence? Who is " the innocent party " in divorce? In many cases one has grievously wronged the other, but dare we say that the other party is entirely blameless? And what of forgiveness? Often it is not even contemplated and yet its healing power is so amazing that it might completely restore the marriage relationship. And what of the children and the chain of results which may follow in them? If they misbehave, who are the real culprits? A boy picks up an apple in a shop. " Put it down," says his mother. " Why? " " Because it's green." An unmarried girl has a baby (there is no such thing as an illegitimate child; there are illegitimate parents). What sort of home has she come from? Have there been discipline and respect for moral standards? We clear the prostitutes off the street, and turn the street-walkers into " call girls ", but we give slight recognition to the fact that the supply is only waiting to meet the demand. There used to be a Women's Offering for the work of Moral Welfare which was chiefly concerned to help unmarried mothers. The truth was not recognised by making it a Men's Offering.

All this does not mean that we should fall into the opposite mistake of saying that the sinner is blameless, like the girl who, after a succession of bad school reports, had to give some explanation to her father and said, " Do you think it is heredity or environment? " The Albemarle Report says (p. 19), " It [society] ought never to remove by anything it does the sense of personal responsibility for their acts from the young." We are far too familiar with some psychologists who eliminate sin altogether until even a child can claim exemption from punishment on the ground that he is maladjusted. It is right because it is merciful to speak of " diminished responsibility ", but there is a real danger that it may tend to remove the sense of responsibility altogether and to focus sympathy on the criminal, so that we forget the victims of violence, sexual offences and even murder. The point is that there is both a corporate and an individual responsibility and the one does not cancel out the other. We can understand why Cain should be asked, " Where is your brother Abel? " But God may also ask, " Abel, where is your brother Cain? " It is a question which we all have to answer when a youngster is sent to penal servitude for beating up an old woman or when he is hanged by the neck until he is dead.

A nation can be guilty of corporate sin. Niebuhr shows that the sin of pride can arise both from a sense of security and insecurity.

In modern international life Great Britain with its too strong a sense of security, which prevented it from taking proper measures of defence in time, and Germany with its maniacal will-to-power, are perfect symbols of the different forms which pride takes among the established and the advancing social forces. The inner stability and the external security of Great Britain have been of such long duration that she may be said to have committed the sin of Babylon and declared, ' I shall be no widow and I shall never know sorrow.' Germany on the other hand suffered from an accentuated form of inferiority long before her defeat in the World War. [Niebuhr writes before her second defeat.] Her boundless contemporary self-assertion, which literally transgresses all bounds previously known in religion, culture and law, is a very accentuated form of the power impulse which betrays a marked inner insecurity. [1]

Pride of race is akin to national pride. We cannot —and must not—ever forget that Hitler did his best to exterminate the Jews and did kill six million of them. We cannot—we must not—forget the Gestapo and the concentration camps and what must surely be the most terrible comment ever printed, " They died in alpha-betical order." [2] To-day we have Apartheid in Africa and even our own country, long proud of offering kind-ness and justice to anyone who makes a home here, has seen with shame racial riots. Storm Jameson, writing of Anne Frank, shows how men can justify the extermination of their fellow men.

The human reason is able to justify any cruelty, by showing that it is necessary, part of a process, a term in a majestic logic—and the rest of it. We used to point to our reason with pride, as proof and glory of our humanity. Reed I may be but I can think. We know now that our reason is capable of anything. Why did Germans bring about the death of this charming, intelligent, good child? Because they had convinced themselves that they had the right, that in destroying her they furthered

[1] op. cit., I, 201, note.

[2] Chester Wilmot, *The Struggle for Europe*. Appendix p. 719, referring to the seven volumes recording the death of 35,318 men, women and children at Mauthausen Concentration camp. " They all died of the same ailment, heart-failure."

aims, a future they had decided to realise. In the end, our pride of intellect, our enlightenment, comes to be weighed in the balance against one child whom we, for our sufficient reasons, have murdered. Dying, of hunger and misery, in Bergen-Belsen, Anne Frank took with her, into a mass grave, every exquisite intellectual structure which allows its servants to torture, to work to death, to kill, for an idea. [1]

Pride of Virtue is another corporate danger. Man equates his own virtues with the virtues of a system. It works like this: " We are keen on this. This is good. Therefore we are good." But the Christian doctrine is that all men are sinful and therefore we must constantly be re-examining our own moral judgments, particularly those which lead us into self-righteousness and the condemnation of others.

We must never commit the error of supposing that because our cause is righteous it therefore follows that we are a righteous people. On the contrary, it is always our own unrighteousness that threatens and menaces the righteous cause that is entrusted to our unworthy hands. . . . There is never any question of God being on our side. The issue for us to consider is always to what extent, and with what degree of depth and conviction, we have placed ourselves on the Lord's side.[2]

Pacifists are prone to fall into this error. One has only to suggest that unilateral renunciation of nuclear weapons

[1] Introduction to *The Diary of a Young Girl*, Anne Frank, p. 11.
[2] *The Bent World*, Langmead Casserley, pp. 215, 216.

is not the only Christian standpoint to be the subject of criticism which is hardly pacific. Pride of virtue may lead to cruelty for the sake of a cause and so to the destruction of the good end we seek.

Pride of knowledge leads to blindness to the will of God and so to corporate Sin. Lewis Mumford sees no difficulty at all in adjusting man's cultural and moral life to the enormous powers available to him. " Impossible? No; for however far modern science and technics have fallen short, they have taught mankind at least one lesson: Nothing is impossible." [1] Educationalists, in this age of specialisation and demand for more and more scientists and technicians, will do well to take warning from this extravagant claim and to remember that life is not made solely by science and technics but involves the whole human personality and our relations with each other. Knowledge does not necessarily bring wisdom; it may lead to the pride which rejects God.

These examples of corporate sin have their origin in the one and same cause, estrangement from God, the Sin of the world. They result in sins against other people, groups, classes, nations, races. But by every sin we wound the heart of our Lord who identified himself with suffering humanity. " For when I was hungry you gave me nothing to eat, when thirsty nothing to drink; when I was a stranger you gave me no home, when naked you did not clothe me; when I was ill and in prison you did not come to my help. . . . I tell you this: anything you did not do for one of these, however humble, you did not do for me." [2]

To be aware of Sin means to be aware of God. First

---

[1] Quoted by R. Niebuhr in *Faith and History*, pp. 80, 81, note.
[2] Matthew 25 : 42 ff.

we must catch something of the majesty and holiness and love of God. When this happened to Isaiah, his first reaction was a consciousness of his own utter unworthiness. " Woe is me! For I am lost: for I am a man of unclean lips, and I dwell in the midst of a people of unclean lips." Secondly, it means that we acknowledge God's absolute claim on our allegiance. " I heard the voice of the Lord saying, Whom shall I send and who will go for us? Then I said, Here I am! Send me." Thirdly, we see that God's will is that we stand or fall as his people, his family. " And he said, Go and say to this people." [1] Everywhere the sense of God brings first the sense of Sin and then, after forgiveness, the sense of vocation and corporate responsibility.

But here we meet a difficulty. What are we to say when thousands to-day have no awareness of God at all and therefore no sense of Sin? When " many citizens, it must be admitted, regard the prohibitions expressly imposed by law as the utmost limits set to their activities and are prepared to take full advantage of any omission or relaxation."? [2] A Saturday Sermon in *The Times* before Refreshment Sunday (the 4th in Lent), when the Gospel for the day is the Feeding of the Five Thousand, asked the question, " Can the Gospel be preached and accepted only as an answer to a conviction of Sin? " This has been assumed in Western tradition. But a sense of Sin is a *religious* experience and presupposes awareness of God. In a religionless world that is no longer dominant in consciousness. All men are sinners, but must they be made to feel that they are sinners before God can speak to their condition? Or can he come to men along different roads? Could it be that some of the trends in

[1] Isaiah 6 : 5, 8, 9.　　　　[2] Wolfenden Report, p. 119.

theology—to an almost exclusive emphasis on the Fall—
may even stand between men and their salvation? The
writer goes on to say that " in the New Testament Jesus
is presented not only as the Saviour from sin but also as
the Divine Word or Wisdom who feeds men with bread
even in the wilderness. This is what men crave to-day,
adrift, as they fear, in a godless universe which offers no
spiritual nourishment, in which life seems to be empty
and meaningless." [1] This is a timely reminder that the
ways of God are as unlimited as his love is boundless.
Our primary concern is our relationship with God. All
human relationships—readiness to forgive included—
depend on this. But we must never put any limit to the
ways in which God may deal with man. He took the
initiative when he "came down from heaven and was made
man." He came to seek and save the lost. The father
who saw his son while he was still some distance off and
ran to meet him, the shepherd who left the ninety-nine
sheep to look for one, may find ways of seeking those
who see no need for forgiveness, no need even for God,
until he finds them.

" As we forgive others." How can we do this? What
will it involve? Can forgiveness take away the Sin of
the world? This is the heart of the matter.

Forgiveness makes very exacting demands on both
parties, the wronged one and the one who does the wrong.
The wronged one has to overcome resentment and
bitterness over the hurt he has suffered. Difficult enough
anyhow, but if hurt pride is the wound, it is the hardest
to heal. If he nurses a grievance, he will increase the
hurt and perhaps wallow in self-pity and in the end do
himself more harm than the original offence did. There

[1] *The Times*, 7th March, 1959.

is no more dangerous poison than refusal to forgive. It may even lead to obsession with the idea of revenge, and " the man that studieth revenge," said Bacon," keeps his wounds green." Jesus even says that the initiative must come from the one who is sinned against. " If your brother commits a sin, go and take the matter up with him, strictly between yourselves, and if he listens to you you have won your brother over." [1] But he also recognises that if the man will not respond, then you can do no more. Jesus says that forgiveness must be unlimited. " If your brother wrongs you, rebuke him; and if he repents, forgive him. Even if he wrongs you seven times in a day and comes back to you seven times saying, ' I am sorry,' you are to forgive him." [2] One remembers as a child reading the story of a boy and girl whose elder brother was unkind to them. They read somewhere in the Bible about " seventy times seven ", so they did the sum and kept a book of offences. And when the score was 490, then they would get their own back. Jesus showed by all his teaching on forgiveness, and by his own example, that any quantitative assessment of forgiveness is as childish and unchristian as this. We ought never to forget that in the Parable of the Lost Son when the son returned to his home—no doubt with lagging feet as he drew nearer—" while he was still a long way off his father saw him, and his heart went out to him. He *ran* to meet him."[3]

But the initiative must also come from the offender because he must repent and be ready to make amends. " I will set off and go to my father, and say to him, 'Father, I have sinned, against God and against you; I am no longer fit to be called your son; treat me as one of your

[1] Matthew 18 : 15.   [2] Luke 17 : 3, 4.   [3] Luke 15 : 20.

paid servants.' " [1] This is repentance and a readiness to try to make amends. It is humiliating to have to ask for forgiveness and this often prevents us from taking the plunge. But if repentance is met half-way, the sting of humiliation is drawn, and this is the test of true forgiveness.

Sometimes people say, " I will forgive but I will never forget." If forgiveness means treating a person as if he had not offended, taking him back as a son and trusting him again, then to forgive but not to forget is a contradiction in terms. We have to dissociate the agent from the evil act, we must not identify him wholly with the evil. Evil is evil and nothing can alter that. The agent is not wholly evil; he is a mixture of good and bad as we all are. There is a real sense in which he alone did not do the evil. We never know all the circumstances and the full chain of responsibility through which a particular evil was done by a particular person. He may be, and often is, more sinned against than sinning. Thus we have to forgive *and* forget.

But can we? And is it right that we should? There are two ways in which forgiveness cannot, and must not, involve forgetting. Forgiveness cannot wipe out the consequences of evil and so remit punishment where it is necessary. The sinner who expects this—and a number do—does not know true penitence, for penitence must include readiness to accept the consequences of sin. Years ago the writer heard a story which he thought silly and immoral, but which in fact is neither. A boy was such a consistent liar that his father adopted the plan of driving a nail into a door for every lie told. In time the boy reacted and turned over a new leaf and his father promised to draw out a nail for every day clear of lies.

[1] Luke 15 : 18.

The day came when the last was withdrawn and it was a great day. The father, however, saw that the boy looked sad and asked him why. The reply was, " The marks show." Yes, the marks do show. A murderer cannot bring his victim back to life; he must pay the penalty. A professional man may be guilty of an offence which brings discredit on his profession. He may have to be expelled from it, never to be readmitted. Hard? Yes, very, but human relationships depend not only upon individuals but on long established standards of honour and reliability in professions and groups and it is vital to maintain their integrity so that our trust and confidence in them may be secure: this is a social necessity. The person must be forgiven and he must not be ostracised by society; but he may have forfeited his place in his profession.

This kind of forgiving but not forgetting is really a safeguard against the dangerous and common fault of condemning whole groups or classes of people because of the failure of some. It is quite unjust, and also quite absurd, to distrust all lawyers because we know of one who has been guilty of unprofessional conduct; to say that the police are corrupt because one has taken a bribe; to call shopkeepers dishonest because one of them has given us short change; to stay away from church because we know of one lazy parson or have read of another who has fallen into grievous sin. This kind of sweeping judgment is of course itself sin because it condemns whole sets of people we know nothing about and identifies them with the evil of which the few have been the agents. It can be seen in its extreme absurdity when people say they will never again speak to a German or a Japanese or a Russian. We cannot, and must not, forget Belsen, the Burma Road and Hungary. But to saddle whole nations with guilt is as silly as it is immoral; and it becomes ludicrous when we include people who were not even born when the evil was done.

The second way in which we must not forget has been implicit in what we have already said. We must never ignore evil. There is a vast difference between forgiving and condoning evil. Jesus forgave the sinner, he never condoned the sin. It was " Go and sin no more." Evil is evil and nothing can make it anything else, and the presence of evil in the world—and especially in ourselves —is too real to be ignored. To forgive by forgetting evil is comparatively simple. It is, in fact, the method adopted by indulgent parents who consistently oppose any attempt by teachers and others in authority who correct or punish their children. It is the way in which " diminished " responsibility becomes no responsibility at all. Humanists and pacifists fall into the same mistake. The former eliminate Sin from their vocabulary. It becomes simply a passing phase in man's development by his own unaided efforts. More education, more science, more hygiene, and everything and everyone will be all right. The latter think that all you have to do is to refuse to use force and everyone will behave like lambs. They "would clutch at universal peace whilst leaving men's hearts still filled with those fell passions which breed war." [1] The real difficulty is not to forgive by forgetting, but to forgive *and* to remember evil. The ultimate object of forgiveness is to cure the Sin of the world.

To say that this is a super-human task brings us face to face with the third great doctrine in this clause of the Lord's Creed—the mystery of the Cross of Christ. No

[1] Hensley Henson, *Theology and Life*, p. 77.

one can explain the Cross though whole libraries of books have been written about it; but we can all understand it. At the risk of repetition we must retrace the steps we have taken; and in doing so we shall draw freely from a profound study of forgiveness and the Sin of the world in *The Kingdom of Free Men* by Dr. Kitson Clark.

" Sin in one man has normally been partly caused by sin in another." [1] Every honest parent knows this. So does every teacher whose school contains a large proportion of children from broken homes. " The fathers and mothers have eaten sour grapes and the children's nerves are set on edge." [2] This chain of responsibility can be seen in groups and nations as well as in individuals. Dr. Kitson Clark gives a telling illustration of how the seeds of the next war may be sown at the Peace Conference of the last. In 1919 the *Daily Herald* published a cartoon showing the allied statesmen leaving the Palace of Versailles. Clemenceau says: " Curious! I seem to hear a child weeping." Behind a pillar is a naked baby in tears above whose head are printed the words " 1940 class." [3]

When we attribute evil to some particular philosophy or economic theory or even to one man, the instinctive desire " is not so much to trace evil to its source in order to eliminate it; it is to attribute guilt in order to punish it." [4] The truth is " that while men can pass judgment on an act, it is beyond their knowledge to pass any final judgment on any individual." [5] Forgiveness is so hard that we try to find substitutes for it and the commonest

[1] op. cit., p. 166.
[2] *The Bent World*, Langmead Casserley, p. 193 (the chapter, " The Divorcing Society ").
[3] Kitson Clark, op. cit., p. 160.
[4] op. cit., p. 169.   [5] op. cit., p. 173.

is punishment. There is an instinctive desire to exact a penalty for wrong-doing. This desire for retribution is not to be dismissed as entirely ignoble, especially not when men are indignant about the sufferings of others; it does recognise the reality of evil. But the trouble is that very often retribution does not cure the evil, but renews it. Our penal system fails to redeem a large number of criminals; total defeat in war with harsh terms on the enemy may cause hatred and bitterness and sow the seeds of another war. Something else is needed to take away the Sin of the world.

" And when they reached the place called The Skull, they crucified him there, and the criminals with him, one on his right and the other on his left. Jesus said, ' Father, forgive them; they do not know what they are doing.' " [1]

" That last sentence ought probably to be written at the beginning of all history books, both as a prayer and as a statement of fact. It is not a denial of the existence and power of evil: at that moment such a denial would have been impossible. Nor is it a denial of the pain, mental and physical, which evil causes. To deny that would also at that moment have been impossible. But that pain was not carried over to the account of those who had caused the evil: it was accepted, absorbed and cancelled by the Judge. By such an action the cords of Sin which bound the world were cut away. I cannot tell you what that means, but I can say this. This is not only an event of eternal importance: it is also plainly an example which must be followed. To try to do so requires all

[1] Luke 23 : 33, 34.

the powers that a man or a woman may possess— all
their knowledge, all their imagination, every nerve
that may be in their body, all their capacity for love
and all their humility, for they must recognise how
much of the evil that is in the world is in their own
minds. Using all these things repeatedly and without
stint they must ask to be forgiven and they must
forgive.[1]

There can be few finer descriptions of the mystery of
the Cross, this miracle of forgiveness, than these words.
We have come a long way and inevitably it has led
us to a green hill far away without a city wall. We have
found that only Jesus can " break the power of cancelled
sin and set the prisoner free." For

> There was no other good enough
> To pay the price of Sin;
> He only could unlock the gate
> Of heaven, and let us in,

—into the Kingdom of Free Men, forgiven and forgiving.

---

[1] Kitson Clark, op. cit., 204 f.

IX. LEAD US NOT INTO TEMPTATION
BUT DELIVER US FROM EVIL

The men who are capable of carrying the burden of their own freedom are very rare.

> Colin Wilson, *Religion and the Rebel*, p. 144

A falling away is of infinitely greater weight than a falling down.

> Dietrich Bonhoeffer, *Ethics*, p. 4

A very common human temptation, to canonize one's own interests. . . . There is also another temptation, the temptation to canonize one's own habits.

> G. Kitson Clark, *The Kingdom of Free Men*, p. 66

An overmastering sense of human ills can be taken as the world's invitation to deny her Maker, or it may be taken as God's invitation to succour his world. Which is it to be?

> Austin Farrer, *Love Almighty and Ills Unlimited*, p. 188

IT WOULD BE A SAFE GUESS that many people find this clause difficult. Their difficulty is that they have a higher idea about God than these words at first sight seem to imply. How can God, who is all good and the source of all goodness, lead anyone into temptation? The suggestion is not only blasphemous, but silly, for God cannot be false to his own nature. St. James says, " No one under trial or temptation should say, ' I am being tempted by God.' " [1] It does not really help us at all to know that the word for " temptation " can also

[1] James 1 : 13.

mean " trial " or " testing ". It is used thus in the
book of Job when the Satan challenges God to put Job
to the test. " Does Job serve God for nought? . . .
Put forth thy hand now, and touch all that he has, and
he will curse thee to thy face." [1] But this is a primitive
idea of God. We can hardly believe that God would put
people to the test merely to see if they can stand up to it.
In the first chapter of the Epistle of St. James the word is
used in both senses. Christians are to rejoice at " trials ".
They produce " the quality of endurance ". But these
" trials " are not just the testing of the book of Job, but
the trials and afflictions that Christians would meet in
the early persecutions and do meet in East Germany
to-day. They may, of course, lead to temptation, but
they are not the direct temptation to *evil* about which
St. James goes on to speak, and which is the subject of
this clause, as is made perfectly clear by " but deliver
us from evil." The real difficulty is that here we are
faced with the words of Jesus. They are part of his
creed and we cannot explain them away.

The clue is to be found, as it so often is, in freedom
with responsibility. To serve God means responsibility.[2]
Constantly God will lead us into situations in which we
can serve him. These will involve choices and therefore
temptations. Every responsibility does. We can only
avoid temptation by avoiding responsibility. When we
accept responsibility we have already overcome the first
temptation of all. The story of Esther illustrates this.
She was the one hope of saving the Jews from massacre.
" Who knows," said Mordecai, " whether you have not

[1] Job 1 : 9, 11.
[2] See the helpful chapter in C. E. Simcox, *Living the Lord's Prayer*,
pp. 71 ff.

come to the kingdom for such a time as this?" The risk, and therefore the temptation, was tremendous, for it was strictly forbidden on pain of death to go to the king unsummoned. Esther accepted the challenge in these fine words, "I will go to the king, though it is against the law; and if I perish, I perish." [1]

Esther was one who had greatness thrust upon her. She did not fall to the first temptation of all. When we have accepted responsibility, we may meet all sorts of other temptations. How shall we use it? Shall it be the easy way to avoid clashing with vested interests or even compromising with what we know to be wrong? Shall it be for popularity, prestige, personal advancement? When Jesus said, "Lead us not into temptation but deliver us from evil" he was surely speaking from his own experience and teaching us to pray as he had prayed. He was "led away by the Spirit into the wilderness, to be tempted by the devil." [2] He was conscious that he had a mission to carry out. He need not have gone to the desert to be tempted at all if he had not overcome the first temptation which was to stay at home where he spent the first thirty years of his life and to turn a deaf ear to the call. Then in the desert he had to face the choices which lay before him—how to set about his work, how to use the powers within him, how to turn men to God. All this is the background which lies behind the prayer.

If we have got to the heart of the prayer, we have found that God will never lead us into temptation but will certainly lead us into responsibilities which may involve temptation. And if anyone thinks that this is a mere quibble or unfair, the answer is really very simple.

[1] Esther 4 : 14, 16. [2] Matthew 4 : 1.

We cannot have freedom without responsibility and freedom is essential to a *human* being. Therefore if we ask to be free from responsibility with temptation, we are asking to be less than human, and that, incidentally, is not freedom at all. Any attempt to translate this clause into a short form of words is pretty hopeless. A paraphrase might run something like this: " We do not ask to be spared responsibility, but we do ask that responsibility may not lead us into temptation. If it does come, deliver us from evil." Or perhaps more shortly: " Let not the challenge of responsibility be an occasion for temptation, but deliver us from evil." Neither is satisfactory, but they may help someone to pray with sincerity and understanding. But far better to use the words we have been given; we shall say them as we believe our Lord meant them and that is enough—enough until he makes his meaning plainer to us as he always does when we go on praying. Meantime we may note that this interpretation of the clause seems to be exactly in line with our Lord's prayer for his disciples, " I pray thee, not to take them out of the world, but to keep them from the evil one." [1] The disciples were not to withdraw from the world and so from the responsibilities and temptations they were bound to meet. But the prayer was that they should be protected from evil by the whole armour of God.

Protected from evil, yes, because temptation is not sin; by the whole armour of God, yes, because there is always a way out. People are often troubled and ashamed because they are tempted, but no one is free from temptation, not even the saints. Sometimes we look wistfully at the really good people and imagine that they are not

[1] John 17 : 15.

like us, exposed to all sorts of temptations. The difference is that they may, and probably do, have different temptations, not that they have none at all. Indeed, the more we advance in the good life and the more sensitive we become to good and evil, the more keenly shall we feel temptation. We may no longer be touched by the more obvious temptations, but there are others which may come in more subtle and dangerous guise, and if we fall to them, the sins which follow may be more grievous. Dorothy Sayers wrote a book called *The Six Other Deadly Sins*. The title was taken from the remark of a young man. " Seven? " he said, " what are the other six? " No, temptation is not sin. The Desert and Gethsemane remind us that Jesus himself was tempted. " For since he himself has passed through the test of suffering, he is able to help those who are meeting their test now." [1] " For ours is not a high priest unable to sympathise with our weaknesses, but one who, because of his likeness to us, has been tested every way, only without sin." [2] Even this can be misunderstood. Some think that it is the experience of sinning which equips people to sympathise with and help others. They would not put it quite like this. They would probably say that when you have tried something you know what it is like and you can learn by experience and help others. But they forget one thing; every temptation resisted means strength, every one to which we fall makes resistance weaker next time. It is not experience of sin, but of temptation overcome, that gives strength. There is always a way out. " So far you have faced no trial beyond what man can bear. God keeps faith, and will not allow you to be tested above your powers, but when

[1] Hebrews 2 : 18.   [2] Hebrews 4 : 15.

the test comes he will at the same time provide a way out,
by enabling you to sustain it." [1] This obviously means
that many a time the way out is to avoid occasions of sin.
It is plain stupid to court temptation. We all have our
particular weaknesses and we know the people, the
things and the situations which may lead us into temptation. Deliberately to run into danger when there is no
need is neither prudent nor brave and there are times
and situations when the way out is to run away. But
this can never mean to run away from responsibility and
the temptations that may go with it. "The first of Jesus'
temptations was an unrecorded one: it was the temptation to avoid temptation." [2] There is a vast difference
between avoiding occasions of sin and shirking responsibility. The point is that God is on our side and he will
lead us and help so that we do not fall into evil.

The question of responsibility reminds us that this
clause, like the rest, is in the plural. I am my brother's
keeper and I must see to it that he too is helped to avoid
occasions of sin. St. Paul touches on this when he talks
about eating meat which had been sacrificed to idols.
He tells the Corinthians that it can be a matter of
complete indifference to Christians.

But be careful that this liberty of yours does not
become a pitfall for the weak. If a weak character
sees you sitting down to a meal in a heathen temple—
you, who "have knowledge"—will not his conscience
be emboldened to eat food consecrated to the heathen
deity? This "knowledge" of yours is utter disaster
to the weak, the brother for whom Christ died. . . .

[1] I Corinthians 10 : 13.
[2] H. Blair, *The Ladder of Temptations*, p. 40.

And therefore, if food be the downfall of my brother,
I will never eat meat any more, for I will not be the
cause of my brother's downfall.[1]

The principle is clear, but it is not always easy to apply.
Why should I curtail my freedom of conscience for someone who has a squeamish conscience? In fact, is it not
my duty to show him that there is no wrong involved?
Yes, we can do this. But the principle remains. We
must not let our freedom be an occasion for a brother
to sin against his conscience, a brother for whom Christ
died.

But we must look further than this. We have to try
to eliminate conditions which are potent sources of
temptation to sin. What of the commercial exploitation
of human weaknesses? Sex and gambling are best sellers,
and we have to admit with shame that the State has
entered the second with Premium Bonds. What about
the dubious night-clubs, salacious literature, violence
depicted in films and on television, suggestive illustrations in advertisements, on posters, and so on? At once
we come face to face with plenty of difficulties. We
have to protect people, especially the young, against
temptations, we have to try to make an environment,
an atmosphere, a public opinion which will deter the
evil and encourage the good. On the other hand, we
have to remember that we cannot make people good by
law. To go too far in the curtailment of freedom and
responsibility may be dangerous. Puritanism is
suspicious of pleasure and may lead to the absurdity of
the man who " once smoked a cigar and found it so

---

[1] I Corinthians 8 : 9, 11, 13.

delicious that he never smoked again." [1]   It can even
lead to pharisaism and sins more grievous than those of
the flesh.   But when all this has been said, there is
plenty of room left for Christian influence and action.
The Christian will first see to his own personal safeguards,
remembering that his own weakness may lead others
astray.   He will also do all he can to eradicate what is
positively harmful in what people see and read and hear.
This is a big field and corporate action is needed.   Far
too rarely do we hear of groups of Christian people
banding together to exert their influence in this way.
But if hundreds of people agreed to boycott a certain
film or refused to take a certain paper or protested against
a television programme, they would achieve their aim.
The purveyors of commercialised vice are very sensitive to
public opinion; their profits depend on it.   But above
all we must protect the young, and in this duty we are,
unhappily, failing badly.   The responsibility rests with
parents, but very many parents to-day are completely
lost.   They expect the schools to do their job for them,
but only too often attack the teachers if they dare to
adopt stern measures.   There is a society for the preven-
tion of physical cruelty to children; we have yet to learn
ways of preventing cruelty to their minds.   Negative
measures and restrictions alone will not do.   In the long
run we can remove temptation and occasions of sin only
by learning to appreciate what is true and beautiful and
good.

If we follow this through, as we ought to, it becomes
clear that culture is a Christian concern.   Writing in
1944 William Temple said that

[1]*Essays in Liberality*, Vidler, p. 99.

the first grave error characteristic of our time is a too exclusive occupation with politics to the neglect of other equally important spheres of human life and activity. It is assumed that the ills from which society is suffering can be cured, if only we have the will and the right aims. It is forgotten that man is not a being ruled wholly by his reason and conscious aims. His life is inextricably intertwined with nature and with the natural associations of family and livelihood, tradition and culture. When the connection with these sources from which the individual life derives nourishment and strength is broken, the whole life of society becomes enfeebled. . . . The real crisis of our time is thus primarily not a moral but a cultural crisis. . . . It must be remembered that when exhortation and suggestion are at variance, suggestion always wins. Christians must take their part in recreating a sound social and cultural life.[1]

This is a salutary reminder that a lot of well-meaning effort may be misdirected and that if a reformation of morals may not be achieved by exhortation, it may be by trying to create a culture which will appeal to the heart of man and draw out his best response. After all, we cannot escape culture, for culture involves values. If we are to try to follow the demands and example of Jesus, we are constantly involved in it. " The alternative seems to be between the effort to reproduce the culture in which Jesus lived, or to translate his words into those of another social order." [2] The former is impossible,

[1] *Religious Experience*, p. 251, 252.
[2] Richard Niebuhr, *Christ and Culture*, p. 82.

for how could we transform the modern world into the social, economic and technological conditions of Palestine of the first century? Thus we are left with the second, and it is just here that the Church is so lacking in prophets and theologians who can interpret the Gospel to modern conditions. But the responsibility cannot be shifted to " leaders " nor can we wait till they appear. If the words of Jesus mean anything at all, every Christian must be as the salt that seasons and the leaven that permeates the whole lump.

" But deliver us from evil." The " but " is important because it connects with the previous clause. Temptation we shall meet *but* deliver us from evil. Whence comes evil? " A man's temptation is due to the pull of his own inward desires, which can be enormously attractive. His own desire takes hold of him, and that produces sin. And sin in the long run means death." [1] " What causes conflicts and quarrels among you? Do they not spring from the aggressiveness of your bodily desires? You want something which you cannot have, and so you are bent on murder; you are envious, and cannot attain your ambition, and so you quarrel and fight." [2] St. James echoes the words of Jesus. " It is what comes out of a man that defiles him. For from inside, out of a man's heart, come evil thoughts, acts of fornication, of theft, murder, adultery, ruthless greed, and malice; fraud, indecency, envy, slander, arrogance and folly." [3] We all know this, but it does not explain the evil. There is, in fact, no doctrine of evil, there is a doctrine of sin. Jesus himself did not explain the origin of sin; he taught us how to deal with it. He did far more; he came to save

[1] James 1 : 14-16. Phillips' translation.
[2] James 4 : 1, 2.   [3] Mark 7 : 21, 22.

sinful men. For there is also a doctrine of " original sin ". The phrase is unsatisfactory. It used to be thought that Genesis 3 was a historical account of the first sin, " the Fall ". All men were thought to be literally the offspring of Adam and so inheritors of his sin. Such an idea is impossible to-day. We have in the Genesis story an old myth to teach the meaning of sin, which is rebellion against God. " The theory did not create the facts: the facts demanded a theory." [1] " Original sin " is the fact of universal sin. " Every man is the Adam of his own soul." This is human experience and the conviction of universal sin led to the Genesis story. " The story did not create the conviction, but the conviction the story." [2] There is a universal tendency to sin for which we are not responsible; there is a doctrine of original sin, not of original guilt. We become responsible and guilty when we commit actual sin. How this tendency originated we do not know, but it must be connected with man's development into a responsible being, free to choose between a higher and a lower, or, quite simply, between right and wrong.

Did God create evil? In the Old Testament it is said that he did, and there is a grain of truth here. But it is so far from the full truth that it is false. We have already rejected the monstrous idea that God can deliberately lead us into temptation; and if it were true that God created evil, what would be the sense of " deliver us from evil "? No, what God did and does is surely this. He creates *human* beings and freedom with responsibility is the hall-mark of a human being. But freedom involves choice and choice means choice between good and evil. We may say that God took a great risk, the risk that

---

[1] Bicknell, *Thirty-nine Articles*, p. 228. [2] op. cit., p. 227.

human beings would choose wrongly; but how else could he create *human* beings, capable of reason, will and love? God respects our freedom so much that he allows us to choose our own destiny. In other words, he created MAN. When people say that all this is unfair, why did God let us be capable of evil, why allow " a problem of evil " and in consequence " a problem of suffering", what they are really saying is, why did he create MAN? There is no answer to that except that God is Almighty love and love demands the giving and receiving of love from beings who are not controlled by force but who are free. So God made MAN.

G. K. Chesterton once said: " If I wish to dissuade a man from drinking his tenth whisky and soda, I slap him on the back and say, ' Be a man! ' No one wishing to dissuade a crocodile from eating its tenth explorer would slap it on the back and say ' Be a croco-dile! ' " [1] This is one way of answering the charge that Christianity gives a pessimistic view of man. The exact opposite is the truth. Man has fallen away from his high estate, his nature is tainted and corrupted, but he is still man. The fact that he has an uneasy conscience shows that sin is not normal to him. He says, " Why did I do it? "; we say, " That's not like him." Thus so far from Christianity painting a picture of the total depravity of human nature, it stoutly maintains that man's true nature is the nature of Jesus. Man's consciousness of sin is proof of his greatness. How and when moral conscious-ness dawned we do not know, but since it is there we cannot call man simply an animal. A crocodile does not know sin. The danger is lest conscience atrophies and so dies. This can come about either through

[1] Quoted in A. R. Vidler, *Essays in Liberality*, p. 40.

failure to develop it or through repeated refusals to listen to it. It is a great mistake to think that conscience is ready-made. We have the faculty of moral consciousness, but like all faculties it has to be developed. Environment and upbringing play their part. We often hear of parents' sorrowful surprise at their children's misdemeanours when they have done little or nothing to provide an environment and example in which appreciation of truth, beauty and goodness can grow. But the will to grow in sensitiveness to good and evil must also be there. To turn a deaf ear to the promptings of conscience will lead to its atrophy. We should be constantly watching to see that we do not become insensitive to evil. It is said that God hardened Pharaoh's heart. He did not, for Pharaoh was free to choose. But God did make the law that insensitiveness to evil must harden the heart. He makes the law, but he makes no one choose. He always respects our freedom. We should also be on our guard against saying that in any man moral consciousness is extinct. It may seem so, but we cannot know. We cannot deny the possibility, but we should be reluctant to think that we have ever known or heard of anyone in this terrible state.

" What a piece of work is man! How noble in reason! How infinite in faculty . . . in action how like an angel! in apprehension how like a god! the beauty of the world! the paragon of animals! " And yet there are times when we may use stronger language than Hamlet's " man delights me not " when we see man's inhumanity to man. The Inquisition and the Innocents, the Gestapo and the gas-chambers, Belsen and brainwashing, the massacre of St. Bartholomew and the massacre on the roads to-day— what a sorry story it all is. Nor is it any comfort to remember that many of these barbarities have been committed by governments wielding " the perilous gift of political power." For governments are a collection of human beings and are often backed by the people who shout, " Not this man but Barabbas. Crucify him."

> They can take a man who was happy and prosperous in the morning and strip him of everything before the evening. They can invade the most loving and united family and scatter them to the four winds, so that its members can never ever learn afterwards whether the others are alive. They can reduce scholars and philosophers till they are nothing more than hungry men fighting for scraps at the garbage pail of a con-centration camp. They can blot out whom they will in a moment.[1]

And then we remember the long roll of men and women who " were too good for this world "[2]—St. Francis and Anne Frank, Elizabeth Fry and Joan of Arc, Shaftesbury and Schweitzer and all those unknown men and women who have died to save others or because they would not break faith with Jesus Christ.

In this book we have purposely avoided any discussion of the text of the Lord's Prayer. We have taken it as we say it. But it is possible that " evil " should be " evil one ". Whichever it is, we can hardly escape asking, Is there a personal Devil? Evil comes from within, but does it also come from without? Is Satan a reality or is the explanation as the child said, " just the

[1] Kitson Clark, *The Kingdom of Free Men*, p. 192.
[2] Hebrews 11 : 38.

same as Father Christmas. It is only father "?[1] Our
Lord spoke of the Devil, but this is not conclusive.
He used the thought of his own day and we do not
know how far his self-limitation as man limited his
human knowledge. But we cannot ignore experience.
There are plenty of people who have been conscious of
a power of evil which seems to possess people. This is
particularly true of missionaries who have often witnessed
a struggle with unseen powers and tell us of the liberating
power of conversion to Christ. These things may be
capable of a psychological explanation. To-day we
should probably describe in other terms those " possessed
by devils " whom our Lord set free. But there will still
remain cases where evil is so manifestly present that it
can almost be felt; and the prudent man will be very
wary of dismissing the possibility of a power of evil, a
spiritual force of evil, which or who is inexplicable except
in terms of a personal devil or devils. However much
mystery remains, certain things are quite clear. First,
whether evil is wholly from within or partly from
without, it is an alien intrusion, foreign to man, unnatural
to *human* nature. Such phrases as " it is human to err ",
" after all it's only human ", " you can't alter human
nature ", are utterly false and mere excuses for sin. What
they really mean is that evil only finds a home in man
and a response from man because there is a universal
tendency to sin. Man sees the higher and finds himself
choosing the lower. " The evil that I don't really want
to do I find I am always doing." [2] Secondly, however
great is the power of evil, the power of good is infinitely
greater. That power *is* personal, for it is God. " It is

[1] Father Andrew, *The Pattern Prayer*, p. 105.
[2] Romans 7 : 19, Phillips' translation.

an agonising situation, and who on earth can set me free from the clutches of my own sinful nature? I thank God there *is* a way out through Jesus Christ our Lord." [1] The Lord's Prayer is the Lord's own Creed. Every clause in it he made his own in his life and experience, and perhaps this clause especially so. At the beginning temptation in a desert, at the end temptation in a garden. Just as the first was a prelude to many a temptation, so the second was the climax of a lifelong victory over temptation. What then are the doctrines inherent in this clause?

First, the doctrine that we are dependent on God. This clause is the humble recognition of that dependence. Phillips translation in the passage just quoted—" Who on earth can set me free—" is significant. Who on *earth*? No one, and certainly not ourselves. It sounds grand to say

I am the master of my fate;
I am the captain of my soul

but it is false. So we pray " deliver us from evil."

Secondly, no doctrine of sin, no problem of evil, can rob man of his freedom with responsibility. Once again we find this doctrine in the Lord's Creed. It is freedom in dependence, the paradox " whose service is perfect freedom ". Thirdly, there is a doctrine of law. God rules by law, and the natural law holds good in the spiritual world. God did not make sin but he made the law that sin spells atrophy and death. Thus there is a doctrine of sin, but not of evil. God is greater and more merciful than his own laws; for Calvary did not break the law

[1] Romans 7 : 24, 25.

that sin means death, but broke " the power of cancelled sin and set the prisoner free." He took the consequences of sin on himself and bore them for us.

It is not strange, but inevitable, that this clause has led us to the same conclusion as the last. Forgiveness and deliverance from evil are both found on Calvary. We shall best understand and best pray both these prayers if our eyes are fixed on the Cross.

X. FOR THINE IS THE KINGDOM, THE POWER AND THE GLORY

While we deliberate, He reigns; when we decide wisely, He reigns; when we decide foolishly, He reigns; when we serve him in humble loyalty, He reigns; when we serve him self-assertively, He reigns; when we rebel and seek to withhold our service, He reigns—the Alpha and Omega, which is, and which was, and which is to come, the Almighty.

William Temple, Sermon at the Lambeth Conference, 1930

> When I survey the wondrous Cross
>   Where the young Prince of glory died,
> Were the whole realm of nature mine,
>   That were an offering far too small;
> Love so amazing, so divine,
>   Demands my soul, my life, my all.
>
> Isaac Watts

> The other gods were strong; but Thou wast weak;
>   They rode, but Thou didst stumble to a throne;
> But to our wounds only God's wounds can speak,
>   And not a god has wounds, but Thou alone.
>
> *Jesus of the Scars, and Other Poems,* Edward Shillito

IN THE TWELFTH CHAPTER of St. John's Gospel there is a very beautiful incident from which William Temple, with his unfailing penetration and imagination, draws out its full significance.[1] It is the anointing of Jesus's feet by Mary at Bethany. Long ago, when she was still " a woman leading an immoral life in the town," [2] she had

[1] *Readings in St. John's Gospel,* p. 189, 190.
[2] Luke 7 : 37.

done the same thing, and the Lord had said " her great love proves that her many sins have been forgiven." " Mary does just what she did before, with only one exception. Then there were tears, but now there are none; for there is no remorse or shame in her devotion now; it is sheer gratitude and love." And then Temple shows that this act has a universal application and significance.

> It is probable that in most of us the spiritual life is impoverished and stunted, because we give so little place to gratitude. It is more important to thank God for blessings received than to pray for them beforehand. For that forward-looking prayer, though right as an expression of dependence upon God, is still self-centred in part, at least, of its interest; there is something which we hope to gain by our prayer. But the backward-looking act of thanksgiving is quite free from this. In itself it is quite selfless. Thus it is akin to love. All our love to God is in response to His love for us; it never starts on our side. ' We love, because He first loved us ' (I John 4 : 19).

There is no thanksgiving in the Lord's Prayer and it is not surprising since it is the Lord's Creed. Moreover the Lord's Prayer is precisely the opposite of self-centredness. It begins with the nature of God himself, it puts as our first duty the hallowing of all that his name stands for and the coming of his Kingdom by the doing of his will, and even the petitions for bread, forgiveness and deliverance from evil are all in the plural and outward-looking, telling us quite plainly that no man is an island, but that we are the family of God. Nevertheless it was

a sound instinct that added the doxology to the Lord's
Prayer. It is indeed " a backward-looking act of thanksgiving." But it is far more than this. It is the acknowledgment that " the Lord is King". There is tremendous
point in the word " for " which follows " deliver us from
evil". He can, he alone can, "*for* thine is the kingdom,
the power and the glory." It is a direct refutation of the
ludicrous claim of the devil—" All this dominion will
I give you, and the glory that goes with it; for it has been
put in my hands and I can give it to anyone I choose. You
have only to do homage to me and it shall all be yours." [1]
Empty boast, hollow promise, impudent temptation, *for*
" thine is the kingdom, the power and the glory." And
yet without the Lord's Creed in the Lord's Prayer it is
a temptation to which anyone may succumb. The
specious promises and the double-talk of Marxist communism fall for it. The self-confident hopes of humanism
fall for it. Power politics and reliance on the deterrent
of fear alone fall for it. Science and technics fall for it.
In fact anyone who worships the wonderful works of
man and forgets the wonderful works of God can do
homage to the devil whilst giving lip-service to God.
But " thine is the kingdom, the power and the glory."
Again and again these words ring out in our prayers and
in our hymns. " Lord of all power and might "; " O
God the king of glory "; " O God the protector of all
that trust in thee, without whom nothing is strong, nothing is holy "; " Jesus lives! to him the throne over all
the world is given."

> Conquering kings their titles take
> From the lands they captive make:

[1] Luke 4 : 6.

Jesu, thine was given thee
From a world thou madest free.

Not another name is given
Power possessing under heaven,
Strong to call dead souls to rise
And exalt them to the skies.[1]

And all this because he is the King of Love and

Love's redeeming work is done;
Fought the fight, the battle won.[2]

We have in this book taken the words of the Lord's
Prayer as we have learnt it and as we say it. The doxology is not part of the original, but no ending to it could
be more appropriate. It is as though we said: " This is
the Lord's Creed in the Lord's Prayer. It is easy to say,
not easy to pray because we cannot pray it unless we
live it. He speaks with authority and therefore we must
obey. Obedience would be impossibly hard but for one
thing—thine is the Kingdom, the Power and the Glory.
It is enough. ' I have faith; help me where faith falls
short.' " [3]

But to return to gratitude. Why are we not more
grateful? Why do we so often omit thankfulness from
our prayers? There are plenty of reasons. Anyone who
tries at all to lead an unselfish life spends a vast amount
of time in serving people and part—an important part—
of this service will be praying for them. Obviously there
are many whom we can only serve by prayer; it is the
only way we can reach them. Thus the Bishop of
Coventry once said, " We may not be able to go to

---

[1] *English Hymnal*, No. 37, translation, J. Chandler.
[2] *English Hymnal*, No. 135, C. Wesley.   [3] Mark 9 : 24.

Moscow on our feet, but we can go on our knees."
" Peter was kept in prison under constant watch, while
the church kept praying fervently for him to God." [1]
It was the only way they could reach him. Thus in this
sense our life is outward-looking and must be so, for how
can a man serve in the sense that Jesus used the word
unless he forgets himself? So it is that we are accustomed
to look forward and not back. Even at night perhaps
we do not review the day, but consider what lies ahead
on the morrow, sometimes with anxiety as to how we
shall cope with it. But we miss something very real,
very heartening, if we do not say " thank you " for so
much given and often so much more than we had dared
to expect. Indeed to review the past and count our
blessings will fortify us for the future; for if I have found
so much so often from so many, need I fear the future
or think it will be less generous with blessings than the
past? There is another good reason for gratitude.
" You will degrade your pity, perhaps you will destroy
altogether the power of pity in you, if you pity yourself.
If there is one thing more humiliating than to say ' How
good I am ' it is to say ' How unfortunate and ill-treated
I am.' " [2] There is plenty of opportunity for self-pity,
and self-pity will destroy gratitude. St. Paul paints a
pretty terrifying picture of the life of a Christian in the
world, but he would not allow one shred of self-pity.

We now can enlighten men only because we can
give them knowledge of the glory of God, as we see
it in the face of Jesus Christ. This priceless treasure
we hold, so to speak, in a common earthenware jar
—to show that the splendid power of it belongs to

[1] Acts 12 : 5.   [2] *The Divine Pity*, Gerald Vann, pp. 116, 117.

God and not to us. We are handicapped on all sides, but we are never frustrated; we are puzzled, but never in despair. We are persecuted, but we never have to stand it alone: we may be knocked down but we are never knocked out! Every day we experience something of the death of the Lord Jesus, so that we may also know the power of the life of Jesus in these bodies of ours. Yes, we who are living are always being exposed to death for Jesus' sake, so that the life of Jesus may be plainly seen in our mortal lives. We are always facing death, but this means that you know more and more of life.[1]

The same thing is expressed in a different way by a Swiss writer, Adrienne Von Speyr.

To be a Christian . . . is a ceaseless undertaking which, as such, is never fulfilled. . . . Within this ceaseless growth is the circle of joy and suffering, the one within the other, neither conceivable without the other—and not merely balancing or neutralising each other (for in that case they would not be Christian)—but both present simultaneously, linked one within the other, in such a way that each and every suffering has its joy within it, or gives birth to joy, and every joy its suffering—(just as a mother's joy over her child is concealed in her pains, and concealed in that joy is the suffering the child will subsequently cause her, and in that suffering again the joy of having suffered for it, each eternally dovetailed into the other). Joy and suffering are the one indivisible form of this ceaselessly expanding life.[2]

[1] II Corinthians 4 : 6–12, Phillips' translation.
[2] *The Word*, pp. 17, 18.

If all this be true to experience—and there are plenty of lives which prove it is—then there can be no fullness of life without gratitude and joy. " The opposite of joy is not gloom, but disillusion, a devaluation of life " [1]; and the opposite of gratitude may prove to be, not ingratitude, but self-pity. It is not surprising that C. S. Lewis calls his account of how he passed from atheism to Christianity *Surprised by Joy*, and that at the head of the chapter " Checkmate ", in which he describes his final conversion, he puts these words of George Macdonald, " The one principle of hell is—' I am my own.' "

Gratitude, then, to whom? To God, of course, and also to others through whom we have so many experiences which help us to enrich life and for which we ought to be profoundly thankful. But gratitude to others does not detract from our gratitude to God, for he gives them to us, he uses them to help us as, indeed, he may use us to help others. God moves in a mysterious way his wonders to perform, but he is heard and seen not only in sea and storm, but in the still, small voice of the lives of holy and humble men of heart, in our friendships and in our chance meetings, in books and newspapers, the radio and television, in all we hear, see and read.

> I hear thy voice, I feel thy wind,
>   The world it is thy Word,
> Whatever wakes my heart and mind
>   Thy presence is, my Lord.[2]

And who is this " My Lord "?

[1] W. Purcell, *The Plain Man Looks at Himself*, p. 47.
[2] George Macdonald, quoted by George MacLeod, *Only One Way Left*, p. 159.

He sent his messengers and we killed them. He came himself and we killed him. There is nothing more that we can do. But he returns from the dead glorious and strong and wholly undiscouraged, and the voice which we thought we had silenced fills the world and pierces the soul. This immeasurable humility and patience, this ability to receive the full impact of hatred and indifference and go on undeterred, is the strongest of the cords by which he draws us.[1]

Yes, indeed, " with cords of compassion, with the bands of love." [2]

Thus without losing that forward-, outward-looking habit which is the key to imaginative, self-forgetful service, we must cultivate the backward-looking habit which awakens gratitude, and which will save us from attributing to ourselves and our own power what God has done. For there are marvels in the lives of all of us, miracles of achievement at which we stand and wonder. We have to make a difficult decision which may affect the whole course of our life. We think, we discuss, we pray, and then, because we must, we turn to our everyday duties. Later decision becomes perfectly clear, and looking back we can see how events have proved that it could not have been otherwise. Thanks be to God. Or we have to face a difficult interview, to break news which will break a heart, to see someone who has wronged us or whom we have wronged, to persuade someone who is aggressive and stubborn. We pray and we go with a sinking heart. But somehow it turns out quite

---

[1] H. A. Hodges, *The Pattern of the Atonement*, p. 40.
[2] Hosea 11 : 4.

differently from what we had expected, and we marvel at the successful result. Our success? No, thanks be to God. And surely too the greatest victory of all, the conquest of the fear of death. No one can tell us in words that this victory has been won. But there are many from whose dying we know the sting of fear has been drawn, who truly illustrate the words of Jesus, " If anyone obeys my teaching he shall never know what it is to die." [1] " It may truly be said that such a man will not ' experience ' death, because, though it will happen to him, it will matter to him no more than the fall of a leaf from a tree under which he might be reading a book." [2] Thanks be to God. These are the wonderful works of God, and when we experience them we are surprised. We ought not to be; we ought to be surprised that we are surprised, for should we not expect them? We have been told to. " He who has faith in me will do what I am doing; and he will do greater things still because I am going to the Father." [3] Christianity is the religion of Great Expectations, but this should never lead us into great ingratitude. God is not a kind of Welfare State God and Christianity is not a utility religion. He is " always more ready to hear than we to pray and wont to give more than either we desire or deserve." [4]

> For the beauty of the earth
> > For the beauty of the skies,
> For the love which from our birth,
> > Over and around us lies:
>
> For each perfect gift of thine
> > To our race so freely given,

[1] John 8 : 51.   [2] Temple, op. cit., p. 147.
[3] John 14 : 12.   [4] Collect for Trinity, 12.

Graces human and divine,
Flowers of earth and buds of heaven:

Christ our God, to thee we raise
This our sacrifice of praise.[1]

For thine is the Kingdom. Here we shall not think of
the Kingdom quite in the same way as we do in " Thy
Kingdom come ". There we acknowledge the trust laid
upon us to extend God's Kingdom that his will may be
done on earth as it is in heaven. Here we acknowledge
the fact of his Kingship. The Lord is King, already, not
will be. He reigns and no one else. He reigns in our
home, our parish, our office, our country. He reigns
" be the people never so unpatient, the earth never so
unquiet." [2] He reigns over Russia and America, Cuba
and Canada, the Strand and the Stratosphere. He is
more regal than any Hitler or Stalin, more truly royal
than any descendant from a line of kings. Of course
there are many who do not know this and would not
admit it. But it is still a fact. It is perfectly easy to say
that this is a picture of a " far-off divine event " and
that it does not look very much as if the whole creation is
moving towards it. It is easier still to argue that people
who do not know that the Lord is King seem quite happy
in their ignorance—as a school report put it, " If ignorance is bliss, this boy must be supremely happy."
But ignorance is not bliss, and to know that the Lord is
King is the firm ground underneath our feet when the
old foundations of faith are shaken and civilisation is in
peril. Always there are unmistakable signs of his Kingship in the lives of people in whom we see the grace of
goodness, the triumph of truth and the beauty of holiness:

[1] *English Hymnal*, No. 309, F. S. Pierpoint.   [2] Psalm 99: 1.

there is also evident the unlovely trail of sin and suffering which ignorance draws with it.

The Lord was never more kingly than when he reigned from the Cross. " Now," said he, " shall the Prince of this world be driven out. And I shall draw all men to myself, when I am lifted up from the earth." [1] That is a fact of history and it is a continuing fact. When Watts wrote his hymn, " When I survey the wondrous Cross ", the second line read, " where the young prince of glory died," but later he changed it to, " on which the Prince of glory died." (The story that he did so in 1745 when the Young Pretender was marching on London is probably apocryphal.[2]) Would that he had not made the change. We are so accustomed—and sometimes to our cost—to the greatest responsibility resting upon the oldest. We might do well to remember that, at an age when to-day few men would accept or be trusted with very great responsibility, Jesus carried a burden greater than any man has ever borne before or since. It was as the young Prince that he carried to Calvary the Cross and the Sin of the world. He had already told his disciples wherein true royalty is to be found. " In the world, kings lord it over their subjects; and those in authority are called their country's ' Benefactors '. Not so with you; on the contrary, the highest among you must bear himself like the youngest, the chief of you like a servant." [3] So he taught and so he lived. His royal emblem was a towel, his royal progress the *Via Dolorosa*, his crown a crown of thorns and his throne a cross.[4]

[1] John 12 : 31, 32.   [2] See Whale, *Victor and Victim*, p. 61.
[3] Luke 22 : 25.
[4] cf. Streeter in *Adventure*, p. 130, " If we must be pierced by thorns, it is more kingly to wear them as a crown."

There is a profound truth in these words: " The merit of his death . . . lies not in the pain, but in the unswerving obedience of which the willing acceptance of that pain was merely the crowning proof." [1] The Kingship of Jesus rests upon this unswerving obedience to the Father's will. And that is our way to " the royalty of inward happiness." Our plain duty is to learn obedience, and often, as with Jesus, through suffering. " *He* learned obedience in the school of suffering." [2]

> Teach me, my God and King,
> In all things thee to see;
> And what I do in anything
> To do it as for thee! [3]

and to be thankful—thankful that I do not have to grope my way in the dark, but have the " light that enlightens every man " and must obey it; thankful that obedience brings its own reward, serenity and peace; thankful that I am never a lonely pilgrim climbing the Hill Difficult or threading my way through Vanity Fair; for

> Thou didst leave thy throne and thy kingly crown
> When thou camest to earth for me.
> O come to my heart, Lord Jesus;
> There is room in my heart for thee. [4]

Thankful, indeed, that thine is the Kingdom, the Kingdom of Free Men.

Thine is the Power. With the Lord his Kingdom and his Power are synonymous; that is not so with men. An earthly ruler may have the trappings of power, but in

---

[1] H. A. Hodges, *The Pattern of Atonement*, p. 29.
[2] Hebrews 5 : 8.   [3] *English Hymnal*, No. 485, G. Herbert.
[4] *English Hymnal*, No. 585, Emily E. S. Elliott.

reality little or none. In this country the monarch reigns but does not govern, but the power of the throne is very great. It is that intangible influence which comes from a high sense of duty and service which has become traditional in our royal house. At the opposite extreme is the dictator whose power ultimately rests on fear and force and who commands obedience but not love or respect. There is all the difference in the world between power sought for power's sake and the power which asks nothing for itself, but seeks only to give and to serve. Temple said that "in Jesus we see power in complete subordination to love." There could be no better paraphrase of "Thine is the Power". And because God is love, we can say that his love is his power, in fact, that there is only one ultimate power, namely love. This is also true on the human plane. St. Augustine knew this when he said, "Love and do as you please." St. Francis knew it when he overcame his horror of leprosy and kissed the hand of the leper-beggar. Elizabeth Pilenko knew it when she took the place of a frightened girl and passed into the gas-chamber at Ravensbruck on Good Friday, 1945.[1] So it has been all down the ages. Wherever men have loved, even unto death, there the power of the Lord has shone forth from their lives, there they have done those "greater things" of which he spoke.[2] And this is surely what the Beloved Disciple meant when he ended his Gospel with these words: "There is much else that Jesus did. If it were all to be recorded in detail, I suppose the whole world would not hold the books that would be written."[3] These books are the

---

[1] See the account in *A Treasury of the Kingdom*, compiled by E. A. Blackburn and others, p. 251.

[2] John 14 : 12.   [3] John 21 : 25.

lives of men and women, lives in which Jesus writes his continuing story, and the title of every one of them could be " Thine is the Power ".

But just as men do not recognise his Kingdom, so they do not know his power, because they think that mine is the kingdom, the power and the glory. This temptation is as old as the hills and as modern as power politics, the Welfare State and the Affluent Society.

> Take heed lest you forget the Lord your God . . . lest, when you have eaten and are full . . . and your silver and gold is multiplied, and all that you have is multiplied, then your heart be lifted up, and you forget the Lord your God . . . lest you say in your heart " My power and the might of my hand have gotten me this wealth." . . . If you forget the Lord your God and go after other gods and serve them and worship them, I solemnly warn you this day that you shall surely perish.[1]

In this chapter, because we are thinking of gratitude and the need for it, we have been stressing the rule of God more than the disobedience of man. We are more concerned with Paradise Regained than with Paradise Lost. But at least we ought to know the consequences of disobedience and to realise what life would be like if the rule of God was totally ignored. There is a terrible warning in an imaginative picture of life in Antioch in the first century A.D., and if only as a warning it is worth quoting.

> In Antioch all too few care much for anything, and therefore few people are cared for much by anyone.

---

[1] Deuteronomy 8 : 11–19.

There seems to be a quite shocking absence of social and even personal compassion. The external arrangements of the life of Antiochans are so good that it seems to be taken for granted that human suffering ought not to exist. When it does nevertheless and obstinately exist, it is as though people regarded it as a kind of unseemly outrage upon the orderliness of life, an outspoken threat to their light-minded serenity, and so they drive it from their minds and forget. They repudiate sympathy, and therefore are without any driving force of compassion. . . . We have everything and create nothing. . . . We specialise in the kind of play which is clever, brittle, and heartless. . . . There is great cruelty. . . . It comes precisely through the unheeding, uncaring nature of a light-minded people, who, having no particular moral standards, deny themselves heights to aspire to or depths to sink to. They condemn nothing and praise nothing and believe in nothing.[1]

And then Luke, who is a Greek and not a Jew and who is not yet a Christian though he is being prepared for baptism, goes on to point the contrast. He tells how deep is the impression made upon him by the Jewish scriptures.

There is the unwearied determination of the Jews to make the whole range of their national life revolve round the idea that they had of God, so that it all takes its colour from him. When they thought of him as vengeful and cruel they themselves became vengeful and cruel. When they thought of him as

[1] *The Letters of Luke the Physician*, Roger Lloyd, pp. 43, 44.

the pivot of social order, they at once produced the Mosaic code of laws. When they began to picture him as compassionate, they came at last to value pity and tenderness. But throughout this history, with its changing and often contradictory conceptions of what qualities were to be found in God, there was one basic quality they always seemed to recognise in him—his energy. The God one finds in these books is a God who is always in action, always doing things. In fact he is a God in whom it is always worth while to believe.[1]

Yes, indeed, not only worth while, but making the whole difference between life energised by the power of God or an empty tale signifying nothing.

Finally, " thine is the glory ". " We *saw* his glory," [2] wrote St. John; and St. Paul added his testimony that they had seen " the glory of God in the face of Jesus Christ." [3] This was the astonishing thing and in two ways. They were Jews whose pride was that they worshipped one God. And yet they put Jesus on a level with God. Secondly, the glory they saw in Jesus was a complete reversal of former ideas. Through Jesus they learnt that the only power in the world is love. They knew that God was compassionate and tender, but it was a new thing to see glory in something helpless with no power to force and drive. It was glory in humiliation. God had " made himself nothing, assuming the nature of a slave. Bearing the human likeness, revealed in human shape, he humbled himself." [4] And so it was glory in service, suffering and sacrifice. The omnipotent

[1] ibid, pp. 45, 46.   [2] John 1 : 14.
[3] II Corinthians 4 : 6.   [4] Philippians 2 : 7, 8.

God had not come to be served but to serve, the Messiah
had become the Suffering Servant, and the King's crown
was a crown of thorns and his throne a cross. Nothing
could be more revolutionary than this. Not everyone
saw the glory of it. It was " a stumbling block to Jews
and folly to Greeks." [1] But those who knew Jesus and
heard his call saw the glory.

Do we? Yes and No. We are perhaps strangely in-
consistent. We like pomp and pageantry and this is
harmless enough. Indeed, in so far as it symbolises law
and order and good government and reminds us of what
is worth while in our heritage, it is good and useful. But
when we deal with things and popular idols, our values
are often awry. Popular esteem and large possessions
may seem glorious, but it may be a tinselled glory and
" even when a man has more than enough, his wealth
does not give him life." [2] In these days when a person
can become a celebrity on the television screen to millions
of viewers, it is not easy to maintain a true sense of value
and glory. On the other hand, a life of humble, devoted,
loving service rarely fails to command respect and
admiration. It may be a Schweitzer or a Florence
Nightingale, a Father Damien, a Shaftesbury, a Kagawa,
a Small Woman or an Elizabeth Fry, or even some priest
or doctor or nurse, known only to a small circle, but
known for the glory that shines from them. But the world
does not always recognise that they are the books in
which Jesus is writing his story and that they " reflect as
in a mirror the splendour of the Lord, transfigured into
his likeness, from splendour to splendour." [3] God has
never left us without witnesses of his glory. The heavens

---

[1] I Corinthians 1 : 23.   [2] Luke 12 : 15.   [3] II Corinthians 3 : 18.

do declare the glory of God, but his inanimate creation is not his chief glory. Whenever we can say, " I perceive that this is a holy man of God, who is continually passing our way," [1] we see his glory. Whenever we see selfishness yielding to service, fear to courage and force to love, we see his glory. But the reflection, however beautiful, is never the same as the reality. There is only one reality, " the Son who is the effulgence of God's splendour and the stamp of God's very being " [2]—Jesus, my Lord and my God.

> Praise to the holiest in the height,
>   And in the depth be praise,
> In all his works most wonderful,
>   Most sure in all his ways.[3]

We have finished what we set out to do, to show the Lord's own Creed in the Lord's Prayer. How imperfectly we have done this, no one knows better than the writer who is very far from thinking that he has discovered all that there is to discover or that he has even done justice to what he has found. For that matter, who would ever dare to make any such claim? No creed is fully revealed until it is lived, and in trying to live the Lord's Creed progress is hindered by many a doubt, many a failure, many a sin. " A man's reach should exceed his grasp, or what's a heaven for? " [4] All one can say is that the Lord did live this creed and is the only one who ever has done so, completely and utterly in obedience to the Father's will. Therefore " thine is the Kingdom, the Power and the Glory." That we can see and know Jesus, enter his kingdom, share his power and

[1] II Kings 4 : 9.   [2] Hebrews 1 : 3.
[3] *English Hymnal*, No. 471, J. H. Newman.   [4] Robert Browning.

in some small part reflect his glory—for this we should be
profoundly grateful. And so

> When all thy mercies, O my God,
> My rising soul surveys,
> Transported with the view, I'm lost
> In wonder, love and praise.[1]

But that is not the last word. Worship is the purest
form of losing oneself, but real worship can never be
complete with wonder and praise alone. There is love
in it, and love will draw from us one consuming desire,
to make known by word and deed the Kingdom, the
Power and the Glory of God, and in so doing to lose
ourselves. Jesus himself said, " If anyone wishes to be
a follower of mine, he must leave self behind; he
must take up his cross and come with me. Whoever
cares for his own safety is lost; but if any man will let
himself be lost for my sake, he will find his true self." [2]
On the last night of Temple's Mission to Oxford in 1931

the moment for dedication and resolve had come.
The hymn " When I survey the wondrous Cross "
was being " roared out " when, before the last verse,
Temple stopped the singing and said: " I want you
to read over this verse before you sing it. They are
tremendous words. If you mean them with all your
hearts, sing them as loud as you can. If you don't
mean them at all, keep silent. If you mean them
even a little, and want them to mean more, sing them
very softly." There was dead silence while every
eye was fastened on the printed hymn-sheet, and
then—to hear Isaac Watts' words

[1] *English Hymnal*, No. 511, J. Addison.   [2] Matthew 16 : 24, 25.

Were the whole realm of nature mine,
That were an offering far too small;
Love so amazing, so divine,
Demands my soul, my life, my all

whispered by the voices of 2,000 young men and
women was (in the recollection of one of them) " an
experience never to be erased from my memory till
the whole tablet is blotted." [1]

Most of us will dare only to whisper, for we have not
found that perfect love which banishes fear.[2] John
Donne knew this when he wrote:

I have a sin of fear that when I have spun
My last thread, I shall perish on the shore:
Swear by thyself that at my death thy Sun
Shall shine as he shines now, and heretofore:
And having done that, thou hast done,
I fear no more.[3]

That was the last sin he had to confess, and because he
asked only that the sunshine of the Glory of God should
never be dimmed, it was already forgiven.

This and this alone, must be our dominant desire.
The young may rejoice in their youth and have their
visions, if they remember their Creator in the days of
their youth.[4] The aged can have their dreams and renew
their strength, if they can make this prayer their own:

Forsake me not, O God, in mine old age, when I am
gray-headed, until I have shewed thy strength unto

---

[1] *William Temple*, Iremonger, p. 378.   [2] I John 4 : 18.
[3] " Hymn to God the Father."   [4] Ecclesiastes 11 : 9, 12 : 1.

this generation, and thy power unto all them who are yet for to come.[1]

> So be it, Lord; thy throne shall never,
>   Like earth's proud empires, pass away:
> Thy kingdom stands, and grows for ever,
>   Till all thy creatures own thy sway.[2]

[1] Psalm 71 : 16.
[2] *English Hymnal*, No. 277, J. Ellerton.

ACKNOWLEDGEMENTS

The author and publishers thank the following for permission to quote from the works mentioned: *The Bent World*: Langmead Casserly, O.U.P.; *The Importance of Being Human*: E. L. Mascall, O.U.P. and Columbia University Press; *Lambeth Conference 1958*: 'The Family in Contemporary Society', S.P.C.K.; *Lambeth Conference 1948*, S.P.C.K.; *Marriage Failures and the Children*: Spencer Lesson, Longmans Green; *Vocation and Ministry*: Barry, James Nisbet & Co.; *In the End God*: J. A. T. Robinson, James Clarke & Co.; *Smoke on the Mountain:* Joy Davidman, Hodder & Stoughton; *The Mystery of the Kingdom*: Bishop Wand, Faith Press; *Readings in St. John's Gospel*: William Temple, Macmillan (permission Mrs. William Temple); *The Hope of a New World*: William Temple, S.C.M. Press; *God and the Rich Society*: D. L. Munby, O.U.P.; *Strategy for Survival*: W. Young, Penguin; *Equality and Excellence*: D. Jenkins, S.C.M. Press; *Christianity and the World of To-day*: Sir Philip Morris, Epworth Press: *The Nature and Destiny of Man*: R. Niebuhr, Nisbet; *Communication of the Christian Faith*: H. Kraemer, Lutterworth Press; *The Pattern of Atonement*: H. A. Hodges, S.C.M. Press; *Letters of Luke the Physician*: Roger Lloyd, Allen & Unwin; *William Temple*: Iremonger, C.U.P.; *The New English Bible*, O.U.P. and C.U.P.